# Featherweights

Oliver Herwig

# Featherweights

Light, Mobile and Floating Architecture

**Prestel**
Munich · Berlin · London · New York

# Contents

## Inflatable Architecture

## Modern Nomads

## Building a World of Bits and Bytes

## Architecture in Space

# The Weight of the World or: The Invention of Lightness in Architecture

Introduction

Architecture is immobile, so they say, heavy, permanent. Anyone who has ever swapped a roof for a piece of fabric, a door for a zip fastener and a bed for a groundsheet will feel bound to disagree. Architecture has always been light, nomadic, flexible and mobile. This is more than ever the case today. High-tech materials are taking the world of building by storm, as multi-functional envelopes—on a scale that no one would have thought possible, from Richard Rogers' Millennium Dome to Herzog & de Meuron's new football stadiums. Mobile exhibition halls, tents and pneumatics have been the hallmark of star avant-garde architecture since the days of Frei Otto. Even quite ordinary buildings use computer-generated façades that seem to float, with optimized load-bearing structures. Solid walls suddenly seem antiquated when confronted with 'fluid' architecture by a practitioner like Greg Lynn. In fact the discovery of lightness simply reflects the change from the industrial age to a service and media society, where speed is the key to pretty well everything. We are in a period of permanent acceleration, with information mobilized as never before. Information architects on the Internet and at their home computers are opening up new dimensions for design engineers. Streams of data and currency go whizzing round the globe, job nomads flit through the world of work, and even architecture seems unable to resist the urge towards movement and lightness. The fantasies of today's architects are going into orbit as they try to burst through the chains of gravity with their floating structures. Space stations like the ISS present on-going challenges for their designers. Architects talk about working "up there," but not just because of the sheer need to survive in space. It is above all a response to the central, ecological challenge of the third millennium on earth: building more and better with less and less.

This book does not set out to be a scientific history of lightweight construction. The aim is to examine the idea of lightness in Modern architecture, and to look at prospects for building in the third millennium on this basis. "Lightness," says Ralf Höller, "always means dynamics conveyed aesthetically."[1] So the book concentrates on aesthetic qualities, bold buildings that caused a stir, broke through boundaries and expanded the idea of what architecture can (and must) do today.

Interest in mobile architecture is increasing, in fact it has led to a minor boom in exhibitions and books.[2] Robert Kronenburg has been particularly involved in this; he recognized and investigated the mobile element in architecture well before anyone else.[3] The present volume takes a different approach from Matthias Ludwig's historical analysis *Mobile Architecture*,[4] Joachim Wilke's purely scientific work *Prozess und Form 'natürlicher Konstruktionen'*[5] or John Pawson's brilliant cult book *Minimum*.[6] It sets out to provide a synthesis that addresses the past as well as the future, and includes the mobile as well as the ephemeral. 'Lightweight' is not a classical category for either architecture or material, and it is not a specific type of building job or criterion for the construction process. It is effective regardless of the materials used, as a space frame, pneumatic structure or even as a concrete shell. For this reason, lightness can appear in various guises: as a finely detailed façade, visually liberated from weight, as a constructional solution, reducing the load-bearing elements to a minimum, or merely as a sketch. Lightness is just as bound up with temporary buildings and hastily knocked-up treehouses as it is with precise engineering structures. Lightness is many-sided, but it can be very clearly associated with individual architects and their buildings when they are trying out something new.

Some of the lightweight designers were heavyweights of Modern architecture. The first part of the book focuses on prototypical designers and structures that helped to shape the twentieth century. In many ways this is an ancestral line of free spirits, five pioneers of lightweight architecture: Bruno Taut, Eero Saarinen, Richard Buckminster Fuller, Ulrich Müther and the Archigram group. They represent various aspects, ranging from the sketches and glass fantasies of Taut the Expressionist on the eve of the First World War to Buckminster Fuller's rational geometry, from the aesthetic appearance of inspired solid building à la Saarinen to Ulrich Müther's socialist shell structures and Archigram's manic eruption into the utopian sixties.

Part two brings together responses to the twentieth century's challenges: mobile architecture in the form of inflatable exhibition buildings, membranes and lightweight materials on undreamed-of scales, thanks to ecological and economical lightweight structures, and to virtual structures emerging from the computer. The prospect of weightless architecture in space certainly opens up a new constructional dimension away from the constraints of gravitation, but it also links back to terrestrial demands—responding lightly and rapidly to future requirements.

## Architecture Must Float or: Discovering Lightness

Under the surface of monumental Modernism lurks another kind of architecture, something almost anarchic that relishes trying to find the key to construction. Such architecture is ephemeral, light and mobile. Its history reads like instructions for progressive dematerialization, from the grand gesture to the reduced structure, from prestigious show to the minimalist façade and from long-lasting materials to ultra-light ones originally conceived for shipping and aviation, or for outer space. Minimalist architecture knows how to give things up: "the disappearance of the joints … highlights the disappearance of the material itself."[7] twentieth-century architecture did not discover lightness by accident: it gives Modernism's much-quoted lack of a home an appropriate image in reality: somewhere to live. Mies van der Rohe's 1946–50 Farnsworth House may float elegantly over its site in the Midwest, but Philip Johnson's Glass House in New Caanan (1949) extends universal space into infinity. Glass everywhere, visual links and transparency. Almost four decades later, Johnson was to abandon dividing walls completely; he built the Ghost House (1985) as a skeleton metal frame with wire mesh. A little more than ten years after that, Shigeru Ban may have come up with the ultimate answer to the lightest envelope question with his Wall-less House in the Nagano prefecture. It would seem that there is no end to the dematerialization of buildings.

The search for "soaring architectural form turns out to be a model that has fascinated us for several decades," wrote Jürgen Joedicke as early as 1958,[8] pointing to the designs of Russian Futurism. It is equally correct to include Antonio Sant' Elia's futuristic machine towns in this genealogy, powerful even as pure sketches, and Constructivism with its filigree steel frameworks, thrusting outwards and revealing the inner life that is usually concealed inside, the load-distribution machinery. Vladimir G. Šuchov's Moscow radio tower made a quantum leap in lightweight construction in 1919. Its mass is 75 per cent less than the Eiffel Tower, and its conical grid structure, tapering towards the top—a hyperboloid segment by segment—into hitherto unheard-of lightweight dimensions. Higher, larger and airier. A second tower of Babel, which remained unbuilt on this scale. Technical innovations constantly impinge on the architectural language of Modernism. So-called engineering constructions show very clearly how beauty can arise from the structure itself. As early as the 1920s, Walther Bauersfeld and the Dyckerhoff & Widmann building company had developed a wafer-thin planetarium dome with a support structure made up of short metal members and joints, onto which concrete was then sprayed. From then on the path forks, leading to Buckminster Fuller's geodesic domes and to pure shell constructions of the kind perfected by Félix Candela, Pier Luigi Nervi, Eduardo Torroja and later Ulrich Müther. Konrad Wachsmann explored a sideline in the form of geometrical space frames:

his model studies for aircraft hangars are massive structures, floating longitudinal lattices on ridiculously thin supports. Wachsmann thought big. His tubular steel frame soared 50 metres into the air on each side and was to have been 240 metres long—and it was infinitely extensible in principle, by the addition of further cells.

Frei Otto and Buckminster Fuller offered competing construction concepts at Expo 1967 in Montreal. On one side was the American's enormous geodesic globe made up of short rods linked to form polyhedrons at the intersection points, and covered with a plastic skin. On the other side was Otto's artificial landscape, a billowing tent roof with steel cables and translucent polycarbonate. This staggering demonstration of virtuosity preceded an even greater revolution in 1968, offering a provocatively simple alternative to ageing Modernism: colourful, cheerful worlds of socializing and committed discussion. "Don't settle down, don't bother about property," was how Gernot Nalbach remembers it. His pneumatic house was intended to be built anywhere with the minimum of effort and expense.[9] It was conceived for a particular reason: the 1962 earthquake in Friaul, Italy. Johanna and Gernot Nalbach were students at the Technische Hochschule in Vienna at the time, and wanted to help the earthquake victims: quickly, simply, and above all at a reasonable price. Their "pneumatic house" used semi-finished industrial products. The walls and roof were each made up of a stretched membrane; floors and ladders provided simple frame construction elements. The whole thing could be transported to the earthquake zone by lorry and erected there without difficulty. The first floor living membrane was supported by steel scaffolding, and floated 3.5 metres above its surroundings. Appropriately enough, the first piece of furniture was an inflatable mattress.

Lightness and mobility, in brief, universal architecture that was not created for a specific place, were abundantly present in the luxuriantly curvaceous balloons of the "revolutionary cells." "Pneumatics and revolution agree well. Both are fuelled by wind and the myth of transcendence,"[10] wrote Marc Dessauce, quite rightly, about the years of P(l)op. The architects of Haus-Rucker-Co were promoting love and a radical expansion of consciousness with their wonderful pneumatic structures, some of which were pulled over the head like astronauts' helmets, others were installations that could be walked into, colourful, transparent survival capsules in an environment that was seen as hostile. While astronauts floated through space attached to space capsules as if by umbilical cords, architects were discovering everyday life and redefining both banal and intellectual matters. This applied to love just as much as to interface or communication: they were looking for a light, contemporary approach, directed against the monotony of Modernism and injecting portable mini-worlds into the world around them, which was itself seen as threatened for the first time. This took the form of portable viruses intended to change everyday life step by step, while at the same time protecting the inhabitants. Regardless of

whether the architects were operating as Archigram, Haus-Rucker-Co or Coop Himmelb(l)au, or appearing together, as happened in 1968 at the legendary Structures Gonflables exhibition in the Musée d'Art Moderne in Paris, the spirit of innovation and of unconditional utopias was flourishing. "Frei Otto was our hero, and Buckminster Fuller, that goes without saying,"[11] Gernot Nalbach remembers. The exponents of pneumatic structures liked to go back to ideas that were already in existence, like Walter Bird's inflatable buildings, for example. He had developed a weather-proof radar dome as early as 1948,[12] and later mass produced this at his Birdair company.

But the new millennium is more inclined to rely on practicability and design quality than ideology. Unlike the visions of the cheerful commune, today's buildings tend to take a more pragmatic approach. However, Richard Rogers' Millennium Dome or Nicholas Grimshaw's greenhouses for the Eden Project in Cornwall surpass even the bravest utopias of those days. Contemporary architects are able to furnish even the anarchic, spherical pneumatic with corners and edges, as shown by Axel Thallemer's rectangular structure called Airtecture, reinforced with "muscles" and able to respond actively to wind and snow loads. Much seems to be more perfect and more beautifully finished than in the 'Sturm und Drang' days of the twentieth century, but more consistent as well. Unlike the Futurists, who praised the beauty of racing cars but then only intoxicated themselves with castles in the air drawn by Sant' Elia, today's architects keep their feet firmly on the ground. They identify opportunities in concrete building tasks. Or they find—or invent—new tasks for themselves. The star Japanese architect Shigeru Ban has committed himself to providing humane emergency accommodation that can be built at reasonable cost. He designs tented cities for the United Nation, and creates emergency housing that gets away from the usual desolate, often cramped reality of mobile buildings.

Of course lines of tradition start to emerge, providing new variations on ideas, and then perfecting them. Werner Sobek's glass cube called R 128 may have some jaunty echoes of the Case Study House programme, but he is also manoeuvring the glass Modernism of something like Mies van der Rohe's Farnsworth House or Philip Johnson's Glass House in New Canaan into the technical world of the twenty-first century. "We are completely convinced that modern buildings must not just be absolutely up to date technologically, they should also be protective of resources, light, transparent and emphemeral,"[13] said Sobek, whose aim is "archi-neering," a perfect combination of architectural aesthetics and engineering performance.

Innovations wherever you look. The computer, hitherto just a quiet assistant with complicated calculations applying to loads and construction, is coming into its own as a creative instrument. Greg Lynn, for example, used programmes that were actually created for Hollywood's special-effects industry to generate variations on his building designs very rapidly. These can then be transmitted to suitable CNC machines that will translate them directly into tailor-made modules. Each item a unique object. To a hitherto unknown extent, the computer can transform fixed working processes and architectural structures, kneading the material for as long as it takes for buildings to emerge as musical variations on a theme. Rapidly, and with almost insolent ease.

## The Triumph and the Tragedy of Lightness

Building follows rules. But anyone who sees the world of building as a game, and boils real buildings down to the size of a playing card, is surely being a little careless. The Munich architectural practice of Allmann Sattler Wappner did just that—and won a lot of sympathy for itself with a card game. This made both built and unrealized projects into a handy pack of cards that could be played like Happy Families. More real, but similarly ironic, was the approach taken by Lluís Maria Vidal I Arderiú with his careful structure on top of the monastery of Santa Maria de Lillet. The Catalan architect stretched a scaffolding passage over this ruin on the edge of the Pyrenees, shifted diagonally against the network of the buildings underneath it. There is a view over the ruins and the valley from two vantage points. The whole structure is made of ordinary commercial scaffolding, painted white against the dark woods. A brilliant variation on the passage of time, light and removable at any time. A scaffolding that doesn't build anything else up, but simply reveals what once was.

Lightness even gets into language difficulties. The problem is that it disturbingly rattles at the very heart of construction, which is something that promises security and permanence, safety and a settled life. Like a building society that has been promising for over half a century: "You can build on these stones." We are all too ready to fall into the trap of semantics. Is earthly heaviness not linked with a "sound argument," with a "weighty contribution" and a "fixed conviction"? Luckily there are writers who define lightness more accurately through their precision and ability to react. Like Italo Calvino, who in his essay *Six Memos for the Next Millennium* [14] demands "Lightness," the lightness of reflection with which Perseus overcame the Medusa, "Quickness," rapid reactions, the ability to respond to changing challenges, and finally "Exactitude," the precise, crystal-clear language of art.

Lightness brings contradictions: mobile is not always the same as light. Nor does light necessarily mean transportable. Exhibition designers have long known how to play with contradictory requirements that often cancel each other out. Quantities like time, material, space, effect and cost have to be optimized permanently. Anyone looking at contemporary stage sets—and seeing how quickly they are fitted up and taken out on tours, or how quickly pavilions or exhibition structures disappear—is unlikely to understand what complicated logistics lie behind such spectacular structures. Size often plays a crucial part in the overwhelming aesthetics of modern stage shows. Edgar Reinhard used 200 tons of steel and 60 tons of concrete as early as 1987 for an IBM exhibition stand that floated five metres above the ground, with a ground area of 850 square metres. It was constructed in just ten days. Such massive exhibition pavilions and stage sets for concerts are so large and weigh so much that they are latently immovable. They have long needed trained construction teams to shift the tons of material. Structural demands also increase with size. Until finally pegs or built foundations provide the necessary stability again. Lightness leads to visual tricks. Not every softly fluent bubble reveals how the forces are set against each other in its envelope, especially since computers no longer hold the formal arbitrariness of architectural sculptures in check.

Transportable structures seem light, but they are still tricky to design. Perhaps this is why they are suitable as built manifestos, as signs of the new. From transport via construction logistics to the necessary anchoring and eventual dismantling, each detail has to be calculated, or at least thought about. The old master of the lightweight structure, Frei Otto, is sceptical about the quality of today's tent halls: he says that top architects are needed to design them, but they are seldom really involved. The biggest mobile halls, at the Oktoberfest in Munich, for example, are "very poor architecturally, and particularly so technically."[15] No one going to the Theresienwiese for this event will be looking for top quality architecture. That is to be found a little further north, on the Mittlerer Ring: the Olympic complex designed by Frei Otto with Günther Behnisch for the 1972 games. A transparent tent roof floats high above the visitors, though its lightness was bought at the expense of steel cables as thick as fingers and massive concrete foundations: a striking structure that was perceived as a symbol of an open society. The lightness goes beyond the homeless quality and insecurity of the temporary. Anyone building lightweight structures will go for high tech and ultra-modern aids. So the idea of lightness remains inextricably linked with the architecture of our day; it is the spring that drives innovation, and it is a permanent laboratory. And it may only be as an airy thought intended to take the weight and seriousness away from architecture, as demonstrated at the Swiss Regional Exhibition, Expo.02. Diller + Scofidio created an artificial cloud that could be walked on above Lake Neuchâtel by atomizing lake water and thus dissolving the built structure, making it invisible and intangible. A refreshing prospect for the third millennium, or even the birth of a new view of architecture from the spirit of lightness? We shall see.

# Five Pioneers
# of Light Architecture

DAS BAUGEBIET, VOM MONTE
GENEROSO GESEHEN

Bergbekrönungen, -bearbeitungen, Täler ausgebaut – wie
im Vorigen. Die Hochfläche am Lugano-See
mit gestaffelter, von oben mosaikartig wirkender
Glasarchitektur bebaut. ~

Flugzeuge und Luftschiffe fahren Glückliche, die froh sind, von Krankheit
Anschauen ihres Werkes befreit zu sein – in seligen Augenblicken. Reise
Reise, das Werk entstehen und erfüllt zu sehen, an dem man als Arbeiter irgen
de mitgewirkt hat! Unsere Erde, bisher eine schlechte Wohnung, werde eine gute

# Building
with Light

## Bruno Taut's
Glass Fantasies

*Kristallhaus in den Bergen*

ganz aus Glaskristall errichtet – farbigem

in der Schnee- und Gletscherregion

Andacht Unaussprechliches Schweigen

Tempel des Schweigens

Weg vom Tal her Kristallmaste sind Wegbegleiter. Sie funkeln in der Sonne und besonders die grössten, die sich im Lichte drehen – Kristall-Standarten – Plateaus für Luftlandungen

»Dieses Kristallhaus soll keine „Krone" sein. Wer kann im All krönen wollen! – – Und keine „Stadtkrone". Bruno Taut durfte nicht das Höchste, das Leere über eine Stadt setzen. Architektur und Stadtdunst bleiben unüberbrückbare Gegensätze. Architektur lässt sich nicht „anwenden". Auch nicht auf Ideale. Jeder Menschengedanke soll verstummen, wo die höchste Baulust, wo die Kunst spricht – fern von Hütten und Kasernen – FLÄCHEN KANTEN WÖLBUNGEN RAUM.

◀ Like a rock crystal shining at
sunrise: this drawing from Bruno
Taut's 1919 *Alpine Architecture*
shows temple-like buildings, utterly
detached from everyday life
(*Alpine Architektur*, plate 17).

Bruno Taut stamped his mark on the architectural world of the twentieth century pragmatically and precisely: he was Magdeburg's municipal building director and also planned the woodland housing estate in Zehlendorf that the Berliners affectionately call "Onkel Toms Hütte"—Uncle Tom's Cabin. Taut's social approach can be followed right through to his famous Hufeisensiedlung (Horseshoe Estate): dwellings linked by a common centre point, a patch of green in the middle of the city. Taut was a successful pragmatist of modern city sociology, but reality always has a counterpart in fiction in his case. His intellectual schemes leave the restrictive elements of material behind them, as though architecture—liberated from constraints and petty rules and regulations—could simply "be." Taut's architectural fantasies circle around pure natural form and crystalline structures, linked with an image that Lyonel Feininger also picked up as the title picture for the 1919 Bauhaus manifesto: a Gothic cathedral, crowned with socialist stars. It seems as though Modernism wants to combine a medieval sense of significance with the most advanced technology to create a social utopia that in its turn inspired Taut to create utopian buildings. He builds wonderful things the likes of which have never been seen, on paper, glass mountain ranges transcending the earthbound quality of the stone masses. Taut's ideas climax again in books, starting with *Alpine Architektur* (*Alpine Architecture*; conceived in 1917, drawn in the following year, finally published in 1920), then moving via *Auflösung der Städte* (Dissolving the

With his Kristallhaus in den Bergen (Crystal House in the Mountains), Bruno Taut created a utopian world to counter the greyness of the First World War, apparently accessible only by airship or aeroplane (*Alpine Architektur*, plate 3).

Bruno Taut sketched his visionary architecture as a light-bringing, redeeming force, intended to unite nature and art, and heal a shattered world (*Alpine Architektur*, plate 10).

The culmination of Expressionism
and a romantic view of the world
at the same time: in Bruno Taut's
*Die Bergnacht* (Mountain Night)
patterns of searchlight beams
open up the darkness, with tem-
ples glowing in their light-cones
(*Alpine Architektur*, plate 21).

DIE BERGNACHT ·

SCHEINWERFER UND LEUCHTENDE BAUTEN

21

SCHLUSS
DES 3. TEILS !

Aber das Höhere wissen ! Das gewalt
ist nichts ohne das Höhere. Wir müssen
Unerreichbare kennen und wollen, wenn
bare gelingen soll. Nur Gäste sind wir a
Erde, und eine Heimat haben wir nu
beeren, im Aufgehen darin und im L

Cities; conceived in 1918), *Arbeit an Zeichnungen* (Work on Drawings; to
March 1920, published in 1920) to culminate in *Stadtkrone* (Urban Crown;
written in 1917, published in 1919).[1]

Taut also featured as a critical commentator for his day, producing
numerous travel reports about New Building in the Soviet Union, articles
about specialist building questions and on architectural theory. Taut developed a way of linking image and writing as closely as possible, for himself
and in his letters to like-minded "Gläserne Kette" colleagues: the pictorial
pamphlet.[2] Taut completely changed the nature of architecture in this compound medium. Things that had never been seen before emerged in his
drawn fiction: astral architecture and crystalline works of art, taking up
natural structures and crystallizing them pictorially as the metaphysical
intellectual worlds of the turn of the century. Taut wants to see a universal
work of art that will unite the world: "Let us construct a magnificent struc-

ture together! A structure that is not just architecture, in which everything, painting, sculpture, everything comes together to make great architecture, and in which architecture is again subsumed in the other arts. Here architecture should be the frame and the content, everything at the same time," he wrote in February 1914 in Herwarth Walden's magazine *Der Sturm*. As a complement to this, Taut developed the idea of "urban crowns," intended to tower up over the great cities, imposing order as monumental centres in the same way as his crystalline mountain summits, the Alps. Taut wanted the built world to be charged overall with eternal values, offering rapt devotion and "inexpressible silence," as he writes in his pictorial cycle *Alpine Architecture*. Anyone seeing this powerful sequence of images will be quick to realize how skilfully the drama is being redefined as part of a piece of redemption poetry. The buildings on the mountaintops float in a fading glow. Writing at the time of the cruel human slaughter of the First World War, Taut manages to disembody these built structures, raising them into the sphere of a spiritual fusion of art and the world, of man and the spirit of the world, of the bourgeoisie, the intellectuals and the workers. His crystalline buildings, striving to the heavens, are signs of a diffuse social utopia, seeking solitude, grandeur and purification in "firns in the eternal ice and snow," as Taut notes on plate 10 of *Alpine Architecture*, "decorated with new constructions, areas and blocks of coloured glass like mountain blossom." Then Taut strikes a sadder note: "It would certainly be enormously difficult to put this into practice; it would need sacrifice, but it would not be impossible. 'Rarely is the impossible asked of man' (Goethe)."[4] But Taut was not aiming for the impossible. In his mind he was piling up a crystalline parallel world, intended to restore confidence to his tattered age. While in the trenches outside Verdun the social order of the continent that had hitherto prevailed was bleeding to death, the "world master builder" was erecting an astral vision of reconciliation. For Taut, architecture and fiction no longer seem mutually exclusive, but mutually dependent. Poetry has seldom been so close to the built world. Inspired by his writer friend Paul Scheerbart, who created new spaces for the world and the mind,[5] Taut himself created cosmologies for life, and counter-cosmologies. The two men's co-operation was not restricted to correspondence, it took shape in the magical glass pavilion of the 1914 Werkbund exhibition in Cologne. A few weeks before the beginning of the First World War this pavilion, dedicated to Scheerbart, vouchsafed a glimpse of a crystalline world, as an alternative design to a reality that was out of joint: a built sketch and at the same time a seismographic and sensitive image of a splintered age.

"Buntes Glas zerstört den Hass" ("Coloured glass drives out hate") the support ring of the Werkbund pavilion proclaimed resplendently, one of six couplets that Scheerbart had inscribed on the building. Taut had built this showroom for the glass industry in record time, only shortly before the Werkbund show opened. Somewhat to one side of the usual exhibition

Thin reinforced steel ribs supported panels of prismatic glass, joining to form a glowing dome above the visitors' heads.

buildings, this domed structure, placed between the ticket counters and the exhibition railway station, soon became one of the show's most discussed landmarks.

The rendered masonry base allowed the ultra-light dome with its network of steel literally to grow out of the ground. Steps led up to the entrance as if to a temple or holy place, and the interior was like a glass palace. Taut, who had already built a pavilion for the steel industry in Leipzig in 1913, was presenting a religious experience of space: areas of prismatic glass spiralled upwards to a dome that inspired the building's nickname: Asparagus Tip. Its phallic exterior was reminiscent of natural growth, but at night the glass prism, supported by fourteen piers, turned into a shining star of technical progress. The experimental structure was lit by electricity, 1,000 glowing watts. Visitors and architecture critics were so overcome by its appearance that they often just stood and marvelled, without paying any attention to details. Plans and numerous photographs of the interior have survived, but none of them are in colour. All modern reconstruction attempts remain speculation to an extent, even though there is a great deal to suggest that Taut chose similar colour combinations as the ones he used for his *Alpine architecture*, in other words "pastel shades."[6] Technology and aesthetics came together in a new way. Taut, working with the utmost sophistication, composed an overwhelming aesthetic of light reflections, waterfalls and cascades, complementing the visitors' movement patterns. He let the curious viewers climb up one side of a grotto and down the other, seemingly passing through layers of glass. The whole structure was an act of refined visitor choreography: while some could move up into the astral hall, others were able to plunge underground into a grotto full of cascades and water features, reminiscent of a

Glass staircases led the visitors to the various storeys between glass walls built of square prismatic lights. These are the stairs leading down from the central dome area to the so-called Ornamentum.

23  Bruno Taut

mysterious cult. There were visual connections between the glass dome, luminous enough to eliminate the outside world, and the underground base. The two levels were linked by a circular opening in the centre.

The whole concept of the pavilion with its lattice dome was based on correspondences. Taut was well aware of the significance of his building in constructional terms as well: "For a building of this kind it is essential that the load-bearing structure is as light as possible, not just for the sake of the overall form," he declared in a 1914 building brochure. "The lattice structure of the vaulting, which deviates from absolute construction form, attempts to do this. The lightness of the building as executed is due to the Allgemeine Beton & Eisen Gesellschaft in Berlin, which was the only one of the firms whose advice was sought to take over the calculations and the practical execution of the designed structure."[7] Metaphor was part of the overall image of this lightweight structure, supported by Scheerbart's poetry, celebrating the glass industry in changing banners. Scheerbart wanted his rhyming couplets to seem "improvised and unaffected."[8] The fact that his most revealing rhyme—"Preise nicht mehr den Luftballon, preise doch mal das Eisenbeton" ("Stop praising balloons and praise reinforced concrete") was turned down did not do any harm to the programme

The extraordinary pavilion was also called "Spargelkopf" (Asparagus Tip). This photograph taken in 1914 shows Bruno Taut's masterpiece; it was exhibited for four weeks only at the Cologne Werkbund exhibition, up to the outbreak of the First World War.

Bruno Taut brought the elements water, glass and light together in the centre of his pavilion to create a sensual and mystical experience for visitors. The water was channelled downwards in a whole variety of forms.

as a whole. Ultimately these were more than advertising slogans. For the rear extension Scheerbart came up with the ironic formulation: "Das Glas bringt uns die neue Zeit / Backsteinkultur tut uns nur leid" ("Glass is bringing in a new age for us / We are just sorry for brick"). But the time was not yet ripe for glass utopias, and Taut had to have his glass structure demolished in July 1916.

"We want lightness, we want to be liberated from the everyday, from things that are easy to teach," was Taut's message in *Glaserzeugung*[9] in 1920, an ambition he had already redeemed in his early masterpiece, the glass pavilion in Cologne. He set (intoxicated) dissolution, cloudy perception and joyful transcendence against war. Taut's combination of social revolution and advanced technology promised a new dynamic for architecture, which had long been looking for appropriate forms to express the new century.

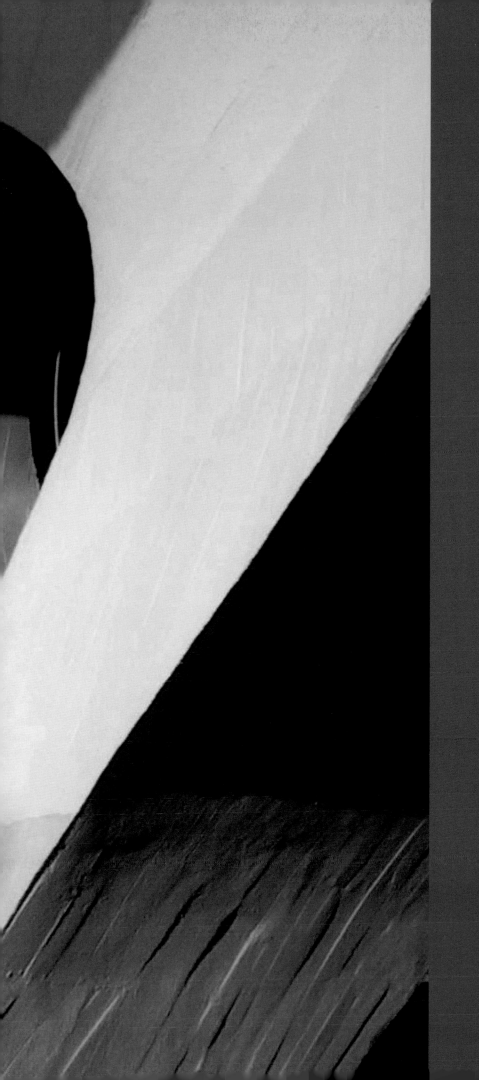

# Light and Heavy

Eero Saarinen's
Trans World
Airlines Terminal
in New York

"Our architecture is too humble," said Eero Saarinen in July 1956, "it should be prouder, more aggressive, much richer and larger than we see it today"—modestly adding: "I would like to do my part in expanding that richness."[1] Large-scale, sculptural form and dramatic impact from a distance play an outstanding part in the American architect's work, reflecting the sense of a fresh start in the middle years of the century. Saarinen thought big and built in the same way, combining free form and rational production processes to create a powerful architectural synthesis.

The twentieth century had moved into a febrile phase. Despite the Cold War, the West was enjoying a tremendous economic boom, which made itself felt in a vibrant and dynamic sense of life. Everything seemed possible. A helicopter in the front garden, a completely automatic kitchen or robots doing the housework. Occasional tables became space-age artworks, and cars were motorized cult object. The limos' tail fins looked more and more like caricatures of the shiny jet planes that were drawing their vapour trails across the sky. Flying radically altered the definition of time and space: journeys that used to take days were over in a few hours to be killed between take-off and landing. Air travel had redeemed the avantgarde promise of high speed and boundless universal spaces to an almost alarming extent. Space, time and architecture were linked in a new way. But flying also made heavy demands on the quality of the infrastructure on the ground and its ability to link horizontal and vertical movement sensibly. Nineteenth-century railway stations had represented a similar quantum leap in transport architecture. Those stations usually hid the new features behind magnificent pseudo-historical façades. It was only when passengers reached the platforms that they found themselves in light-flooded halls. These were advanced engineering structures, cast-iron vaults of hitherto unknown dimensions, providing the right setting for the trains as they steamed in and out. But Modernism threw restraint to the winds. Airports were to combine logistics and aesthetics to create their own formal

◄ Eero Saarinen's terminal for TWA in New York was the epitome of movement for a whole generation. Y-shaped piers thrust the roof upwards effortlessly and dynamically, and also make it possible to provide enormous panoramic windows.

language even on the outside; Eero Saarinen was ready to deliver this. With his stopwatch in his hand he got his colleagues to race about and capture the rhythms of the passengers' movements so that he could base the building on them: spacious, transparent, dynamized spaces, enlivened by steps, perspectives and curved roofscapes intended to put the passengers into the right mood for their journey. Even though the terminal buildings had to stay on the ground, they at least had to try to convey the feeling that they were shaking off the constraints of gravity. Two icons of transport architecture came into being in quick succession: the theatrical Trans World Airline (TWA) terminal in Idlewild, later New York City's JFK airport (1958–62) and the ingenious Dulles International Airport outside Washington, D.C. in Chantily, Virginia (1958–63).

Proud, aggressive and large—Saarinen's dictum sounds like a declaration of war on a self-consuming Modernism for which he felt new

It's almost too good to look through: the panoramic Window on the World is an eye-catching feature in its own right. The glass panes are supported by a fragile steel structure.

challenges had come. Saarinen was born in Kirkkonummi, Finland on 20 August 1910. Now 46, he had already won contracts to design some striking advertisements for the USA, his monumental Jefferson Memorial in Saint Louis and the competition-wining embassies in London and Oslo. He was responsible for some self-confident buildings in Europe, but these did not yet show the ambitious architect at the height of his powers. Saarinen's work marks the shift from the first generation of Modernism, peaking with Le Corbusier and Mies van der Rohe, on to the next one, which of course addressed the achievements of the Bauhaus and the International Style, often formulating critical statements of their own about them. Eero Saarinen had moved to the New World with his father Eliel, who had won second prize in the Chicago Tribune Tower Competition in 1922. He left crisis-torn Europe a year later with 20,000 dollars in his pocket to seek his fortune in the States.

The father-and-son practice attacked the New World's great building demands with almost military precision, working on factory and research projects of hitherto unheard-of size. The General Motors' Technical Center in Warren, Michigan came into being from 1951–57. This was a mega-project demonstrating the ambitions and determination of a world concern whose products were to make a great impact on the post-war period. Eero Saarinen was no exponent of the Beaux-Arts tradition like his father, who, throughout his life, remained committed to a proto-Modernism that was as monumental as it was craft-based. Eero was a modern architect through and through, always determined to be in the vanguard of development. His own education was comparatively conventional—as a sculpture student in Paris (Grande Chaumière 1929–30) and an architecture student in Yale (1931–34), Saarinen had a strong sense of modern architecture, and this left Mies's Illinois Institute of Technology Campus in Chicago as the only relevant model for the GM Technical Center. Saarinen's ability to go straight to the heart of design problems rationally, to dissolve building masses into two dimensions or make them into a concentrated presence also helped him with subsequent industrial projects. Both the Bell Laboratories in Holmdell, New Jersey and IBM's Thomas J. Watson Research Center in Yorktown, New York produced the kind of industrial mega-architecture that had long since taken over from great country mansions. Saarinen approached the Trans World Airlines Terminal in Idlewild in the light of his experience on these mega-projects. Airports had become the symbol of their day, the twentieth century's very own building commission, embodying Modernism's technical acceleration and its mobility to an equal extent.

Aircraft come in and go out, at least in pilots' language. The TWA terminal was intended to have just the same inspiring effect on its visitors, as a vigorous spatial continuum and structure that thrust out expressionistically on all sides. Even today the photographer Ezra Toller, whose shots fundamentally shaped our perceptions of the terminal, still talks about a

"wonderful exploitation of the plastic quality of concrete."[2] As a trained sculptor, Saarinen was determined to transform his terminal into a dynamic, large-scale sculpture and to break up the concrete envelope, which all too often stood for mass and solidity, with bands of light, giving them a disturbing, soaring quality. The building was intended to redefine dynamics and construction. The architect seemed to be flattered by his contemporaries' determination to see the theatrical outward thrust of the terminal building as a soaring bird, even though he rejected it firmly: "The fact that to some people it looked like a bird in flight was really coincidental," Saarinen likes to point out: "That was the last thing we ever thought about. Now, that doesn't mean that one doesn't have the right do see it that way or to explain it to laymen in those terms, especially because laymen are usually more literally than visually inclined."[3] Saarinen was well aware how symbolic, indeed seductive, the roofscape with its total of four segments sailing above the glass façades must seem to the observer. The concrete roofs of the terminal stretched out in all directions like a larger-than-life compass card, the perfect symbol of Trans World Airlines as a global transport company.

Was Saarinen really only trying to embody abstract ideas, with no reference points in the real world? Or did he simply take pleasure in seeing his architecture turning into a symbol of flying as such, into a great bird spreading its wings? There is a legend that describes the architect playfully turning over an empty grapefruit half; he pushed the centre in and was suddenly holding the shape of his terminal in his hands. However

Up, up and away. Under the four protective shells of the terminal building, stairs, railings and bridges are composed to make the last few yards before joining the aircraft into a major drama of arrival and leave-taking.

A delicate bridge spans the space, forming a symbolic gateway that passengers must pass. Here at the latest the journey begins.

The information pod is like a futuristic guardian figure giving information about arrivals and departures. It is clear how Saarinen stage-managed the joints of the four shells as bands of light.

brilliant this creative act might sound, the reality was very different. Countless models were made in the development phase. The commission was a milestone for Saarinen, who carried out endless studies to test the load-bearing capacity of his design and its spatial consequences. Ultimately the great master-builder wanted a structure "in which architecture itself would express the drama and specialness and excitement of travel."[4]

The entrance to the building was already an overture to this. As you got out of your car, you approached the apex of a triangular porch thrusting out into space, supported by two Y-columns holding up three concrete shells. The two load-bearing elements look massive, but they soar dynamically out of the ground and draw the eye further towards the boldly formulated concrete shells. These have glazed windows underneath them that mark the interior like filigree curtains, rather than closing it off. The TWA Terminal has a logic all its own. Saarinen's "total environment" promises control over every piece of design and every niche. This was the only way in which he could achieve the "fullest impact and expression."[5] The terminal looks like a rejection of the right angle. Spaces flow into each other, piers grow out of the ground, visitors are taken up by the surge and carried on. People walking through the glass ellipse feel as though they are in a moving installation directed at the airfield, a shadowy presence beyond a flight of stairs and a second glass curtain. Visitors are immediately confronted with the information pod, keeping an eye on the entrance like a watchman. From here there is only one direction: up. Wide curving stairs lead to the Main Lobby. You go under a filigree bridge and see stairs at the side, rolling back like long curls. The passengers are finally rewarded with a fantastic view of the stands, the two satellites and the airfield.

Saarinen did design an interior that was 13 metres high, and enlivened with dramatic perspectives and curves, but in fact at a length of just under 100 metres its dimensions were very manageable. The architect simply put up a gigantic "umbrella" over the passengers, though its shape does not illustrate the flow of forces within the structure. On the contrary: rather than going for an aesthetic of thin shells and engineering, Saarinen chooses the dramatic path. He designs according to his own ideas of form and the statics experts have to use every trick in the book to stabilize this expansively gesturing building. Saarinen's roofscapes "were deliberately chosen in order to emphasize an upward-soaring quality of line."[6] Saarinen may not have wanted to conquer gravity, but he did want to get the better of it: "We wanted to counteract the earthbound feeling and the heaviness … We wanted uplift."[7] Saarinen was well aware of the dramatic style needed to do this, the dynamic spatial sequences and the visually optimized load-bearing members: "For the same reason, the structural shapes of the columns were dramatized to stress their upward-curving sweep."[8] No wonder Saarinen identified the Baroque style and its spatial perception as the model for his TWA building.[9]

This powerful presentation worked. Pictures of the lounges, bars and restaurants still convey the impression of another world, with passengers and staff moving as though they are in a grand opera. Steps soar upward to the first floor, where the Paris Café and the Lisbon Lounge offered their guests tubular steel chairs and elegant armchairs from Raymond Loewy's practice: a romantic and elegant preparation for air travel. "Drama" and "excitement" were the key concepts for which Saarinen created his great stage. And at the same time he sculpted the space in order to come to terms with man's ancient desire to fly. Saarinen espoused the cause of movement and transition: "We wanted the architecture to reveal the terminal, not as a static, enclosed place, but as a place of movement and transition."[10] Paradoxically, even though the building's only function seemed to be to channel streams of passengers, his choreography of the lines of movement gave New York's airport a fixed point. And that was precisely what chaotic Idlewild needed from the outset. Every airline was supposed to have its own terminal, which led to competition between individual buildings that cut brutally across the masterplan for a "Terminal City," which had proposed a loose but consistent series of check-in buildings around the circular access road.

Saarinen said on the building site on 17 April 1961: "TWA is beginning to look marvelous. If anything happened and they had to stop work right now and just leave it in this state, I think it would make a beautiful ruin, like the Baths of Caracalla."[11] It was his last visit to Idlewild. Less than six months later, on 1 September 1961, Eero Saarinen died of a tumour in Ann Arbor, Michigan. He left behind a whole series of incomplete projects.

An exclusive experience for the few: travellers in the sixties in the spacious, almost empty terminal, with its surging ups and downs seeming to anticipate the beauty of flight.

Overall Saarinen's work was too scattered to convey a consistent picture of his ideas. And things do not look any different for the TWA Terminal today. The building is now no longer used, and faces an uncertain future. Now that the days of elegant long-distance travel are numbered, this architectural icon seems like a fossil that will have to fit in with future megastructures at JFK airport, as a restaurant or a museum of a bygone era.

Ten projects were carried out by the practice partners after Saarinen's death, some by the chief designer Kevin Roche who himself went on to be a well-known architect. Saarinen had started on a large number of building commissions at the same time in his later years. The TWA Building was followed by Dulles International Airport outside Washington, D.C. The fluent, open, Modernist space that Saarinen had sculpted in New York had given way to a cooler vision. Suspended between two gigantic piers that look like an ancient temple from a distance, a concrete roof spans a column-free space that looks open to almost unlimited expansion on either side. A final point. Both Saarinen's airport projects accepted the most advanced technology of his day and responded to it with works of the same calibre. He combined monumental qualities with the ephemera of his streams of visitors, and the moving space with a sense of lightness that was intended to help the passengers to soar even before the actual flight.

# Geometry: Go and No-Go

# Richard Buck-minster Fuller's Visions

"The Dymaxion American" was *TIME* magazine's cover title for its Richard Buckminter Fuller issue on 10 January 1964. This story made the 69-year-old overnight into something that the Harvard drop-out and subversive inventor had long been in the eyes of his contemporaries: a modern legend. Dymaxion, coined from dynamic and maximum, promised maximum efficiency in almost every sphere of construction, and Bucky, as his fans enthusiastically called him, was soaring effortlessly on the spirit of the age. His bold ideas and equivalent architecture gave his age the crucial light-weight note it needed to break out of the constraints of gravity and send people into orbit and finally to the moon.

Buckminster Fuller was never lost for words; his construction credo also allowed for creating the world through language. As a creative force who used his special way of talking—"thinking out loud"—not only to develop complex thought edifices, but also to plant ideas in his listeners' minds at the same time, he extended Modernism's machine metaphor on to a global scale for the first time, down to his *Operating Manual for Spaceship Earth*, the title of his most popular book. Everything fitted together. And the conceptual cosmos that he erected around his structures functioned like an elastic putty that sealed off even the tiniest gaps and stabilized projects by embedding them in a consistent view of the world. "Connecting" was the magic word. Bucky collected insights from scattered fields of knowledge and used them as aids for new projects. In contrast with the figure of almost 200 lectures delivered per year by Buckminster Fuller for a time, the number of buildings he realized seems relatively modest. Each is unique in its field, however similar his geodesic domes may be. Their Tensegrity ("tensional integrity") structure makes them seem light, a system made up of tensile-stressed elements—the cables—and pressure-loaded elements—the spars.

Buckminster Fuller was a master of concretizing abstract thoughts. His mathematically precise structure at Expo 1967 looks like a Euclidian diagram from a maths book. But Bucky was also good at embedding concrete things within a broad frame of reference. Whether he was inventing the metaphor of "spaceship earth" or real buildings, Buckminster Fuller was rarely satisfied with his improvements to detail. He was also not shy about marketing his comprehensive design philosophy. As in the case of the so-called Dymaxion House, the famous neologism that an enthusiastic advertising manager of Marshall Field's department store in Chicago invented when Buckminster Fuller showed a model of his 4D House there in 1927: an unconventional dwelling intended to be exhibited pretty well anywhere in the world.

It may be surprising at first sight, given how fresh his ideas are, that Buckminster Fuller, who was born in Milton, Massachusetts on 12 July 1895, really wasn't one of the younger designers when he made his break-through. But it fits in completely with his indirect route into the world of building: he didn't start his career as a designer and architect until 1927.

Buckminster Fuller liked to sell himself: in 1958 he demonstrated how light so-called Tensegrity structures made up of rods and cables can be, even though they are perfectly viable as stable load-bearing structures.

◄ Buckminster Fuller's boldest plan for a prominent location was a dome over Midtown Manhattan. It was placed like a gigantic shimmering bubble between the Hudson and East Rivers, reducing skyscrapers and even the Empire State Building to a toy backdrop.

Home, sweet home for Anne and Richard Buckminster Fuller: the Home Dome in Carbondale, Illinois flaunted its qualities by providing a residence for the great inventor and his wife.

Bucky, who was involved in the creation of 240 structures"[1] between 1922 and 1927, looks back with horror on the "chaos in the building trade and the world of improvisation in housing construction,"[2] offering something in place of that chaos: order and a systematic approach, down to the last detail. The programmatic Dymaxion House (1927), a hexagonal metal structure, summed up his new lightweight aesthetic: it is functional, radically simple, systematic and economical, as it is serially produced. A product that still looks futuristic today, an autonomous artefact that can be assembled on site in the shortest possible time, fitted with its own energy supply and drainage pit and the most advanced media technology: easy to manufacture, easy to transport and assemble and just as easy to demolish again. The architect had thought of everything, from the distribution of the radially arranged rooms down to the furnishing of the individual segments, which were suspended from a central mast and seemed to float freely in the air. Buckminster Fuller loved compact, space-saving, multi-functional ideas. This extends from the washing unit, which was reminiscent of the way ships' cabins are fitted out, down to the cupboard, whose inner workings are like a rotating conveyor-belt with a whole variety of drawers. Buckminster Fuller's understanding of mobility also made him look for appropriate vehicles, cars and aircraft, which a second model dating from 1929 shows in front of the actual building. This pipe dream of a house planned in advance down to the last detail and open to systematic

A wonderful mixture of sailing-boat and tree-house: the model of Buckminster Fuller's Dymaxion House was supported by a central mast and floated freely in the air. Car-space was provided under the living platform.

The first building phase for the Witchita House: a bundled-tube mast was built on point foundations. This carried the ring network with its characteristic thrust collars, which was then covered with thermofoil and aluminium.

In an advanced building phase the ventilator is placed on top of the circular living-machine assembled from prefabricated parts—a crane lifts the aluminium top on to the opening provided for it.

assembly did not come true. Not because no one would have been interested in this strange phenomenon in the rectangular world of American timber houses and trailer homes. But because the "most famous prototype of a prefabricated house"[3] got caught up in the maelstrom of the 1929 world economic crisis.

"Fortunately" Buckminster Fuller was not an architect—an unintentional irony in the chairman of the Architectural League's introduction to Fuller's talk about the Dymaxion House on 9 July 1929. Harvey W. Corbett was clearly struggling for words to describe the Buckminster Fuller phenomenon: "He is not an engineer either. He has none of the attributes we know. But he started to think about housing construction, about the kind of clean machine that is entirely appropriate to housing needs."[4] Anyone reading Buckminster Fuller's lecture, which is as fascinating as it is discursive, will sense how he is trying step by step to undermine the legitimacy of existing architects so that he could present his model as the only logical one, and be aware of the threat that this self-trained loner was offering to the establishment. Buckminster Fuller made a general attack on the existing world of construction. The non-architect insisted that in the Dymaxion House "there is nothing that corresponds to our current approach to building."[5] No production of "meaningless archaic forms,"[6] just pure lightness. Fuller gives the weight of the Dymaxion House as 6,000 pounds, and he estimates that the cost for serial production would be 3,000 dollars. A strong man could lift the rafters without difficulty. Buckminster Fuller did not fail to provide any answers, but his lightweight house did not get any further.

This did not happen until 1944. A UFO-like circular structure made up of prefabricated aluminium sections landed in the Midwest, in Kansas, as though it had fallen from the sky. Buckminster Fuller's Wichita House took up principles of the Dymaxion model and developed them as a serial product. The exterior façade was made up of thermofoil and aluminium, arranged around a central mast and a ring lattice with various thrust collars set into it. This was an unusual project, and Buckminster Fuller had an equally unusual ally. Rather than a conventional trailer-home firm the aircraft manufacturers Beech, who were familiar with lightweight construction principles, agreed to co-operate. The Wichita House prototype was assembled by 16 men in two days. 37,000 orders were received, but the planned mass production of 250,000 per year never happened, allegedly because Buckminster Fuller refused to "hand over responsibility for the design."[7] Years later he explained that the time had not yet been ripe for prefabricated housing. Instead, Airstream's Silver Bullet caravan bowled along the American highways from 1935, as a gleaming incarnation of mobile architecture—streamlined, light and elegant.

This restless spirit's breakthrough came—how could it be otherwise—from the motor industry. Buckminster Fuller roofed an existing inner courtyard on the Ford factory site in Dearborn, Michigan, with his new

ultra-light structure for the company's fiftieth anniversary in 1953: the geodesic dome contained only a hint of architecture, and yet it triggered a
whole new chapter in construction. Transportable and almost weightless,
and yet extremely stable and with a high load-bearing capacity. This first
commission confirmed the value of these constructions, which had been
developed from 1947. They were made up of linked octahedrons and tetra-
hedrons, and could span enormous areas at minimal expense. This was
because never before had an inventor addressed the world as a whole so
intensively so that it could be copied on a small scale: it came quite naturally to Buckminster Fuller to link a number of areas of knowledge and
practical insights acquired by experimental and empirical research. His
lightweight domes conquered the world, set up and enormously popular in
their hundreds, indeed thousands as climbing frames, emergency accommodation, radar stations and even as homes. These lightweight structures
were a perfect implementation of what Buckminster Fuller stood for: intelligent architecture that could be manufactured in large quantities following
the rules of industrial production and despite all the general enthusiasm
about technology, anticipating the ecological and solar energy movements
by decades.

Buckminster Fuller, who was 58 years old by now, went for broke.
And won. In 1967 an amazed public celebrated the US Pavilion at the Expo
in Montreal, which was 76 metres in diameter. Its creator wanted to show a
different America in his network of struts—a super-power with an eye on
the world, true to the motto "Creative America." The five-eighth sphere
seemed to have a life of its own—individual segments responded directly to
the sun by opening and closing—making the whole thing seem like a structure that could reconcile technology and nature. Buckminster Fuller's filigree pavilion was based on logic and mathematical calculations that made
it possible to handle tensions and loads evenly throughout the structure
and stabilize the whole thing. Bucky's work on even more complex space
frames shows that he intended to go even further.

"Nothing in the universe ever touches anything else" said Buckminster Fuller's patent application, poetry and daring in equal parts, that he
submitted for the Tensegrity structures from 1959 to 1962. The fascination
his geometrical rod structures made up of tensile-stressed cables and
pressure-loaded rods held for architects lay in the visual opulence of the
fragile, apparently floating structure. In fact this was a complicated assembly with low safety margins for the system as a whole. If a single part
failed, the whole structure would collapse, which meant that it was artists
rather than architects who took up Buckminster Fuller's idea. The same
can be said of the calculated fusion of aesthetics, technology and nature
in Buckminster Fuller's domes and rod structures. In the light of this, the
encomium on the occasion of Buckminster Fuller's honorary doctorate
at the Minneapolis College of Art and Design in 1973, when Fuller was 78
years old, seems appropriate: "For Buckminster Fuller, the artist whose

It only took Buckminster Fuller five
weeks to top the rotunda of the
Ford factory in Dearborn, Michigan,
originally planned for the 1933
World Fair, with a dome 28 metres
in diameter.

A filigree steel network of triangles and octahedrons forms the basis for the massive domes that Buckminster Fuller built of minimum materials. He produced his most spectacular geodesic dome for the 1967 World Fair in Montreal. It was 76 metres in diameter, and dedicated to his wife Anne.

studio is Planet Earth, whose materials are the mysteries of the universe, whose aim is to discover the truth, whose motivation is love, whose justification is founded on the vision of a hope that has the future of mankind as its object."[8] This future had already begun, if only with a full-blooded energy crisis.

Ocean liners, aircraft and functional industrial buildings had stimulated emergent Modernism to even bolder structures, and thus shaped the machine aesthetic of the twentieth century, but Buckminster fuller's filigree domes, as in Baton Rouge, Louisiana (repair hall for the Union Tank Car Co.) had abandoned the slightest hint of heavy industry. The subsequent Expo dome and Walt Disney's plagiarized dome in sunny Florida go another step further; they represent a changed leisure society that is not even intimidated by mega-structures like roofing mid-town Manhattan if there is enough profit in it. Bucky's slogan "to do more with less"[9] had changed to its opposite. And the light element of architecture had grown into a gigantic bubble that could burst at any time.

This sparkling jewel 91 metres high seemed to come from another world: the American Pavilion with its automatically controlled blinds symbolized an optimistic future in which technology and nature belonged together.

Master of the
Universe

Archigram's
Pencil Revolution

The cover of Archigram's first monograph in 1972 positioned the most popular innovations—Walking City, Cushicle—in optimistic, candy-bright, kitschy surroundings.

The name was a manifesto: Archigram, an abbreviation for "architectural telegram." They were to shake up the rigid architectural landscape of the 1960s, and then take it by storm. And open up new perspectives. Archigram became the epitome of speed, a free ticket for bold designs and for unconventional ideas that had not yet been fully validated. This was all done with a wink, cheerfully, destructively and with a refreshing lack of respect. Archigram was provocation personified. On the title page of the great 1972 monograph,[1] Warren Chalk, Peter Cook, Dennis Crompton, David Greene, Ron Herron and Mike Webb introduced themselves as spherical balloons and exponents of a floating architecture who were magically changing the world beneath them.

The six architects, born between 1927 and 1937, were in their mid-twenties or mid-thirties, ready to question the foundations of architectural Modernism and to pillory the abortive developments of soulless urbanization. Their preferred resources: paper and scissors, imagination and ironic headlines. Archigram was not just the name of a group of like-minded people, it also stood for colourful pamphlets, collages, architectural drawings. The Archigram members, even though they were practising architects with various firms, appeared mainly as media artists in their publications, virtuosi of the spectacular appearance.

Their publication was called the same as the group: *Archigram*. Nine issues appeared between 1961 and 1974. Archigram was related to Monty Python's Flying Circus in its style and presentation, but it did have a serious aim: breaking down and changing conventional approaches to life. Archigram thrived on the visual power of its designs, half ironic collage and comic-book, half a serious instruction manual for a new way of seeing, detached from the constraints of reality. Archigram subjected that reality to a complete metamorphosis, with the aim of making it more colourful, more

lively, but above all more human. To this end, Archigram freed themselves of the ballast of the built world and went on to a different, fundamentally lighter medium: the manifesto. This is exactly what these colourful publications were: drawn declarations of war on the establishment. Enthusiasm for technology, belief in the future and child-like dreams of omnipotence were ironically pushed to the utmost as high-tech mega-structures, using coloured pencils and collage. The Archigram architects combed Modernism like archaeologists for clues that might help them, ready to follow unfamiliar paths and fresh trails. They also recognized the signs of subliminal civilization conflicts in science fiction comics. So we should not be surprised that they took these colourful bubble-worlds at face value, and tried to use space technology to solve the problems of the modern city, for example with bright space-capsule homes docking on to high-rise space stations. In any case, some of the popular designs, deliberately rebelling against the laws of statics and reducing current housing concepts to absurdity were definitely not of this world. Examples are Ron Herron's 1964 Walking City or Peter Cook's Plug-in-City project, devised between 1962 and 1964.

The idea of the Walking City seems so simple that you wonder why no one had thought of it before. Archigram simply gave the city legs. Other people remained tangled up in metaphors of the city as an organism, seeing roads as arteries, but Ron Herron developed the idea of a living, mobile city moving forward in gigantic telescopic strides. The image of a lot of cities connected by tubes stalking up the Hudson River past the skyline of New York City became famous, even though it is not clear whether it is set after a nuclear holocaust. The cities march past Manhattan, the icon of Modernism, unmoved, like a herd of migrating wild animals. These eight-legged creatures with their countless decks are reminiscent of nautical architecture; the massive glass domes formed a strange mixture of fascination with technology and a new closeness to nature. This ambivalence was a feature of many of Archigram's designs. The technical sphere became a playground for lasciviously stretching women, as in the Capsule Home, a cross between a space capsule and a container, or it became a second nature in its own right—capsules growing wild on the 1965 Capsule Pier.

The 40-storey buildings march past the Manhattan skyline like a herd of gigantic migrating animals. Ron Heron's 1964 masterpiece Walking City plays with the idea of mobile architecture.

EACH WALKING UNIT HOUSES NOT ONLY A KEY ELEMENT OF THE CAPITAL , BUT ALSO A LARGE POPULATION OF WORLD TRAVELLER-WORKERS.

# A WALKING CITY

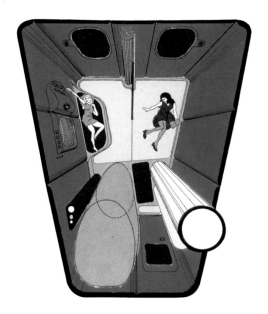 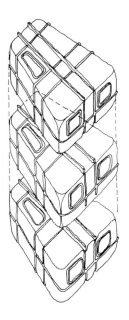

Comfort for you in a space capsule. Two women loll lasciviously in Warren Chalk's Capsule Home (1964). The containers have an integral bathroom (bottom left), pneumatic lift (bottom right) and portholes, and are stacked and plugged in to a central mast radially.

Rowhenson. 1964.

Peter Cook logically thought through the concept of the mass-produced world in his Plug-in-City. Individual residential modules docked with the mega-structure, where they were stacked, placed in rows and related to each other. Or they were uncoupled again, detached from the housing machine, which was rather like the North Sea oil platforms. A simple crane lifted up the individual cells, then grouped them around itself as if in a gigantic container terminal. The world of housing remained flexible. And Archigram offered a general plan for the "further refinement of the organization of big cities,"[2] which were like moving organisms, at the same time taking Modernism's analogy with machines and cars literally.

Blow-out-Villages and Instant City were among Archigram's most fascinating creations: a short picture cycle demonstrated the idea in the style of a comic strip: a hovercraft arrives and looks for another development location. With its great telescopic mast in the middle and arms at the sides it is like a fairground attraction. And in exactly the same way as a fairground attraction, it offers dynamism. The arms are raised and unfold. Platforms float in the air, stages that can be constantly re-arranged and used in new ways. Finally an inflatable, membrane dome, supported only by air, unfolds above the star. A new world has come into being. "Mobile villages," Peter Cook explains, "can be placed in any location where people are looking for new accommodation after disasters, for workers in remote areas and as leisure complexes, either as permanent buildings or out of season at the seaside, or at festivals."[3]

Instant City (IC) worked in a similar way. Peter Cook's comic strip calls it "a sleeping city." And the scenery remains flat, as befitting sleepers. All that is to be seen is a zeppelin on the horizon, like a rising sun. The first inhabitants notice something: "Hey, look at that," someone shouts from the

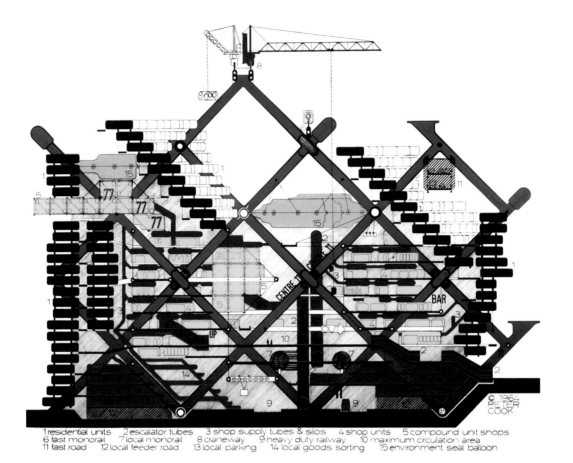

1 residential units    2 escalator tubes    3 shop supply tubes & silos    4 shop units    5 compound unit shops
6 fast monorail    7 local monorail    8 craneway    9 heavy duty railway    10 maximum circulation area
11 fast road    12 local feeder road    13 local parking    14 local goods sorting    15 environment seal balloon

office building window. Cut. Scene 2: "Descent." The balloon makes fast, puts out its feelers and links up with the city. Cables and anchor-ropes, a canvas is unfolded. And the airship travellers disembark directly above the town hall, conquering the scene. The local IC headquarters already has a aerial, the equipment has already been accommodated. Cut. Scene 3: "Event." The transformation is well under way. The sky becomes an open-air cinema, the square becomes a theatre, the ice-cream runs out (Archigram always go for sensual experience and direct participation). Cut. Scene 4: "Highest Infiltration." The people are organizing themselves independently, the city is no longer the same. Cut. Scene 5: "Infiltration." The pale outlines have been filled in with life, information tables and action groups announce a new beginning. The ugly office block has acquired a weird and wonderful dome, and the IC information centre seem to be well established. The balloon disappears. Cut. Scene 6: "Network takes over." The interlinked city makes contact with others of a like mind, the zeppelin is disappearing over the horizon, on its way to new sleeping cities. The principle is the same as the one for the Blow-out-Village: movement, development, transformation.

"Learning from Las Vegas" was a Postmodern slogan.[4] Archigram learned from comics, from the colourful future worlds of science fiction, directly adopting its style and vague projections of the future, backed by a

Section through the 1964 Plug-in-City: Peter Cook's Plug-in-City offered growing, constantly changing structures whose living units can be freighted like containers. "The Plug-in-City is set up by applying a large scale network structure, containing access ways and essential services, to any terrain," was Archigram's definition of the project.

single major aim: change. Archigram had nothing less in mind than this, a cheerful mixture of rainbow, sunrises (here they were entirely comparable with Bruno Taut's *Alpine Architecture* graphics cycle) and people. Even though only an infinitely tiny proportion of their work was realized, Archigram remained the pulse generator and condensation nucleus for all the malcontents tinkering away at alternative worlds. For example, it is said that Richard Rogers' Millennium Dome in London was based on some of Archigram's ideas about ephemeral architecture. But there is an exhibition machine that made the British high-tech dream come true in a much more striking way. The Georges Pompidou Centre in Paris, loved by visitors from all over the world for its wonderful views of Paris and the external escalators with a space-ship look, boiled down a great deal of what Archigram had campaigned for. A city-centre refinery that actually looked as though it had fallen out of the sky with its technology-loving exterior and completely flexible interior life. It would probably never have become reality without Archigram's pioneering designs. And yet a certain dissatisfaction remains. However light Archigram's world might seem, in retrospect it shows both how Modernism aged remorselessly after 1945 and also how today's Utopias are fading. In the wild world of the sixties a great deal seemed possible without needing to prove itself feasible: capsule homes or even walking cities. Archigram was a child of its times, which shows not least in the anachronistic choice of a word for its technical reference medium—the telegram. Indirectly, another association offered itself as well: an ark, promising rescue from the monotonous mish-mash of mass housing and soulless building projects. And a secret affirmation of what has been playfully questioned. After all, they were not called Anarchigram. Their rebellion, which consciously used extra-terrestrial resources, fizzled out because it was too preoccupied with human forms and less with people's real needs. Peter Cook, for example, devoted himself to teaching. Thus more and more pragmatism was mixed into the project. Instead of removing the limits on what could be built only in his own mind, he planted the desire to change in the minds of new generations of architects.

Pop-Art goes architecture. No wonder that Archigram struck like a meteor in the 1960s. The group focused a broad protest movement against the establishment that could suddenly be sensed everywhere: Hans Hollein, Coop Himmelb(l)au or Haus-Rucker-Co in Austria, as well as the Japanese Metabolists or the pneumatic worlds of Jean Aubert. A great deal could be achieved, radical change was on the agenda, a desire to shake off the ossified constraints of Modernism and to risk making a new start socially. Archigram's architectural visions soared to hitherto unheard-of heights at the peak of this movement.

# BEFORE IC: A SLEEPING TOWN

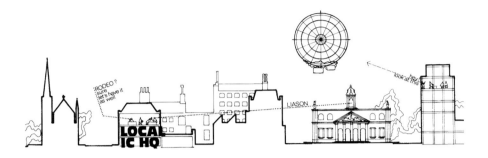

# DESCENT

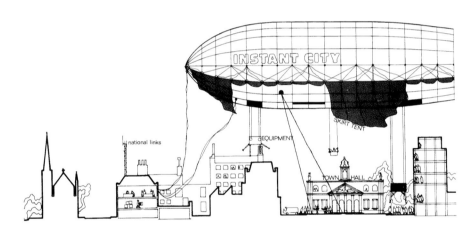

# EVENT

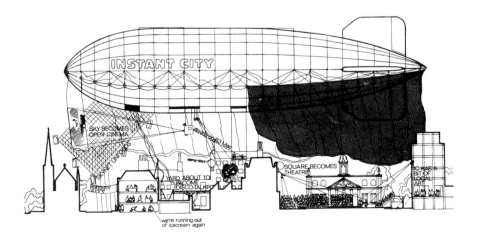

Change is in the air: Peter Cook's vision of Instant City Airships (1970) transformed the typical English town by linking up its infrastructure medially, forming a centre and involving the inhabitants themselves in the design process. Here there are clear parallels with the protest and grass-roots movements of the late sixties, which saw architecture as a democratic decision to be made by a city and its residents.

# HIGHEST
# INTENSITY

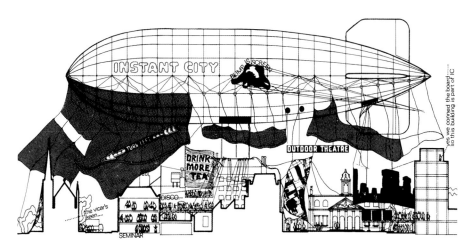

# INFILTRATION

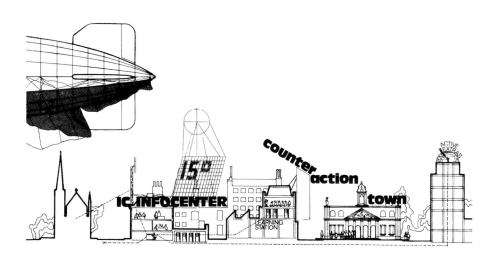

# NETWORK
# TAKES OVER

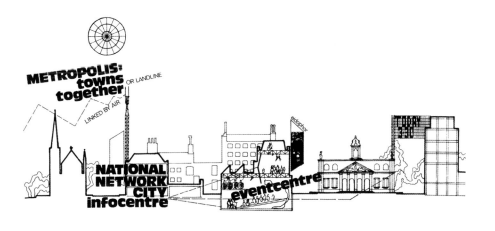

Escaping from
Slab Construction

Ulrich Müther's
Shell Artworks

"The best thing that happened to me was the Ahornblatt being pulled down," says Ulrich Müther, "That got me back on the scene."[1] This is because a piece of (building) history disappeared with his Berlin restaurant in August 2000. And the focus suddenly shifted to the GDR architect who had almost been forgotten. About 200 articles fulminated against this crime against architecture. Müther's spectacular 1973 shell structure, not far from the Berliner Dom, was summarily demolished to make way for a speculative development. In fact the Ahornblatt with its widely protruding roofs—the finest concrete shells, fragile products of Socialism—was the built family silver of the Workers' and Peasants' State: exotic even under the GDR, a non-conformist, rebellious building, completely out of place in Berlin's block periphery grid after reunification.

Müther went sailing while the demolition diggers were breaking up the delicate shells. Why should he watch that? Even the shell constructions that remain—about 50 of them—are living dangerously. It is not their unusual construction method, it is the times that are gnawing away at them. Inselparadies, a former excursion destination in Baabe on Rügen island is fading quietly away, its windows broken and boarded up. And Müther's first building, a hypar shell for the Haus der Stahlwerker holiday home, for a time the Hotel Vierjahreszeiten in Binz, was simply pulled

◂ The 1967 Music Pavilion in Sassnitz is definitely one of the most unusual buildings of its kind. It consists of a shell-shaped cantilever arm with a radius of ten metres and two flanking wings.

Five hyperboloid segments spanned the so-called Ahornblatt (Maple Leaf) in central Berlin. This restaurant built in 1972–73 was pulled down in July 2000, despite vigorous protests.

A bus-stop with a difference in Binz. This hyperboloid shell spans seven metres but its walls are still only 5.5 centimetres thick. All the glass inserts have been removed so that the bold curve of the shell can make an even greater impact.

down. The building itself was listed, but not its shell, says Müther gloomily. This is a race with the ravages of time, which has no taste for non-conformist buildings. Today the 68-year-old master builder of shells keeps the records from his office—files, folders and documents from over three decades of professional practice—in his own archive in Prora. The fact that the mammoth National Socialist KdF (Kraft-durch-Freude [Strength through Joy]) leisure complex should be housing the records of the GDR's most advanced master builder sounds like history's *esprit de l'escalier*.

Müther built his first shell in 1963. At first he had thought of using plain barrels for the steelworkers' building. But a college friend announced cheekily: "What are those old wagons supposed to be, you need Candela shells for that!" Félix Candela, the Spanish-Mexican architect born in Madrid in 1910 became a leading light with his thin-walled concrete shells, and not just for Müther. Echoes of the bold hyperbolic paraboloids that Candela introduced to architecture and put thoroughly through their paces crop up all the time in the Binz master builder's work. For example, his Ahornblatt is reminiscent of Candela's restaurant in Xochimilco and even the graphic appearance of "his own firm," the VEB Spezialbetonbau on Rügen, quotes with its dynamic roof from the church of San José Obero in Monterrey, built by Candela in 1960.

But Müther, a trained carpenter and mechanical engineering student from the Technische Hochschule in Dresden added something else as well. He did not just want to build, he wanted to do the calculations for the structure himself. And so he spent 14 months on mathematics for his diploma thesis on hypar (hyperbolic parabaloid) shells, curved surfaces that can be constructed from straight shuttering. Calculating this geometrical shape without the aid of a computer was a hard nut to crack. Müther went about it "with a certain degree of stubbornness," until even his diploma supervisor felt he had to agree to the ambitious task. "You simply won't let go," said his professor, resigned yet delighted.

Actually Müther wanted to be an architect. But as the son of an entrepreneur he didn't fit in with the Workers' and Peasants' State's image of society, and so couldn't get a college place at first. He had to earn one as a craftsman—only workers were admitted to extramural courses. Müther struggled to get through here as well. Of 180 students starting the course, only ten gained their diplomas according to plan. The architect is convinced that this was an "élite corps," somewhat reprehensible for a state that was fanatically committed to equality. Müther's fluent forms also went against the architectural grain in the GDR. The rectangle was the norm, the ideology demanded conformity. But the son of an architect from Binz was not prepared to go along with this. Even when the family business was expropriated and turned into the PGH Bau Binz Müther did not give up. As the elected technical director of the co-operative he was still in charge of how things went. Müther was elected for a year on each occasion. And this happened for twelve years in succession. In 1972 the concern was turned into a VEB—a state owned business—but Müther remained its director. In his quiet but determined way he made a (technological) niche for himself: spherical shells using a further development of the gunned concrete construction method. This used no shuttering, concrete was simply sprayed on to a fine-mesh net—ideal for planetariums all round the world and one of the GDR's rare export hits. Its creator lived and worked far away from the centres in Rostock, Schwerin and Berlin, on the shores of the Baltic. Of course he had lived well off the beaten track, Müther said, but this had not harmed any of his enterprises, quite the contrary. Müther could manage things much as he pleased in a small business. To a certain extent he could also decide about staffing, and bring in the team he wanted. News of his success was quick to spread in the GDR, so that there was no lack of motivated and experienced colleagues. Experimental design using suspended models and subsequent testing of the structural statics using tensile strain measurement on his shells was a regular additional feature, after construction and calculation using algorithms and Robotron computers.

"I will build that for you," said Müther forcefully in 1968, when he landed his first major commission, which was to design for the Teepott, a tourist restaurant in Warnemünde. His confidence was justified, as he had the means of production as well as the ideas, a rarity in an economy beset by shortages. He had had a monopoly of high-quality gunned Torkret concrete machines for some time. He had relied on this capacity when designing the sweep of the protruding roofs for the Teepott. It looks expressive and experimental, and is well suited to its beach location. The broad canopy roofs protect its huge glass façades from the summer sun, without needing any elaborate system of shades, blinds and fabrics, which would have reduced the view of the dunes and waves. The restaurant is well placed strategically on the beach at Warnemünde, at a point where there is

The Teepott unfurls its 1,200 square metres of roof area, more delicate than the finest porcelain. This shell construction, which is seven centimetres thick, was built in Warnemünde in 1968. Behind it is the lighthouse dating from 1897–98.

a sharp bend in the promenade, which then runs straight towards the box that is the Hotel Neptun. Müther built his round structure here, right next door to the historic lighthouse of 1897–98. The alterations carried out in 2002 did not leave a great deal of the building's sense of space: it used to be possible to look straight out under the three curves in the roof from the balustrade on the first floor. The monolith was trimmed back to accommodate the realities of capitalism. Several tenants now use the building, with additional structures and dividing walls that break up the former spatial continuum. You can only form an impression of the lavish overall Teepott complex from the lighthouse now. It is like a gigantic cloverleaf, with its three roofs thrusting out into the landscape through an angle of 120 degrees.

Here comes "the young rationalizer from Binz": this was how the Communist party functionaries greeted Müther when the spectacular restaurant opened. The year was 1968, the positive mood of early socialism was showing the first signs of fatigue, and the comrades were enthusiastic about this architect without party allegiances. Müther had planned and built this prominent structure by the sea in just 210 days, working with the architects Erich Kaufmann, Carl-Heinz Pastor and Hans Fleischhauer. A concrete shell only seven centimetres thick spans about 1,200 square metres of roof. "You're right up with the fashion here," was the comment on the shell structure by a functionary. Prime Minister Willi Stoph, himself a trained mason and constructional engineer, was pretty amazed when he saw the building in all its sweeping impudence, Müther remembers.

Müther transformed socialism's notorious shortages into design achievements at the highest level. His VEB Spezialbau Rügen was responsible for pleasure in the GDR. The company built restaurants and exhibition

Ulrich Müther's bobsleigh run, built in Oberhof in 1987, catapulted the GDR into the winter sports' world league.

Baywatch on the Baltic. The life-guard station in Binz shows Ulrich Müther's shell skills in the late seventies. The station looks out over the dunes like a one-legged UFO on the watch for pretty mermaids.

halls, cafés and music pavilions with poetic names like Baltic Pearl and Water Lily, Maple Leaf or Island Paradise. He also designed the architectural emblems of the socialist enthusiasm for sport: swimming pools and cycle racetracks, and also developed the technology for the famous bobsleigh run in Oberhof—1032.89 metres of concrete bends, made without shuttering in cement gun concrete. A sensation. So then the engineer from Binz was always in demand when special structures were needed. His range extended from buildings for competitive cycle training to roofing for swimming pools. The pinnacle of his achievement was the planetariums that he planned and exported with Zeiss of Jena: to Finland, Kuwait and Libya, and to the nearby Federal Republic of Germany, where spherical shells almost 20 metres in diameter were built in Wolfsburg and elsewhere. Müther points out that once you know the projection technology represents only ten per cent of the building total, you will find it easy to understand why Zeiss was so interested in joint marketing.

Ulrich Müther was often asked about the secret of his success. He replied tersely that he had learned it from the sons of Pomeranian farmers: "Work hard and don't say much." Müther came from a family of architects and ships' captains, and so it is not surprising that he saw parallels with shipbuilding. It is not just that the materials are the same—synthetic resin reinforced with glass fibre, for example—but so is the underlying aesthetic. If something looks beautiful to a shipbuilder, it will also sail across the sea well, lightly and fast. Anyone walking along the promenade in recently renovated Binz and seeing the seaside villas with their traditional wooden balconies, swiftly put in place following the old patterns, will suddenly be confronted with a foreign body: Müther's 1968 lifeboat station in the dunes. It is a ferro-cement shell structure on a base, rising a little higher than a man over the green of the shore. It was built with the Binz architect Dietrich Otto, and looks like a jacked-up car, gently rounded, with

A socialist export hit, and not just in the heat of North Africa: Ulrich Müther's 1979 Spacemaster planetarium in Tripoli, Libya, consists of a dome 17.8 metres in diameter and five flanking shells.

High-tech and ornamentation are not mutually exclusive. One of the shell structures flanking the 1979 planetarium in Tripoli, Libya.

panoramic windows on all sides. It was constructed in two halves that were then joined together in the middle like the shells of an oyster. You get inside via a flight of steel steps, a modern cave, combining a whole range of phenomena: the low ceiling, the view over the sea, more light than you need and landscape under your nose.

If you wanted paper-thin concrete shells in East Germany, there was only one man who could do them: Ulrich Müther, whose socialist workers' and peasants' icons have been having a hard time since the fall of the Wall. Whereeras elsewhere the industrialized construction world became a sequence of things that were all the same, slab-constructed "workers' lockers," Müther retained a speculative element in architecture, elegant and enormously light.

There he stands against the Baltic sky, a tall, lanky figure in a dark suit. His tie is perfectly tied, and his close-cropped hair makes him look like an artist. And he reminds you of the highly ethical achievements of the "mathematically and statically gifted" local master builder from Binz: modest, ironic and full of very dry remarks. "It's a bit like watchmaking," is Müther's comment on his thin shell structures. And then when he screws his eyes up he really does look like a Swiss craftsman enjoying the struggle with a tricky problem, someone who still tightens even the tiniest screw with his own hands and puts everything into delivering his masterpiece.

# Looking Ahead.
# Light, Mobile and
# Floating
# Architecture

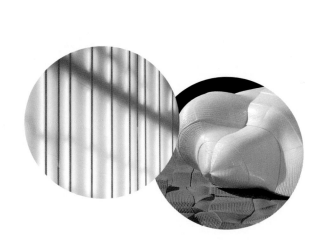

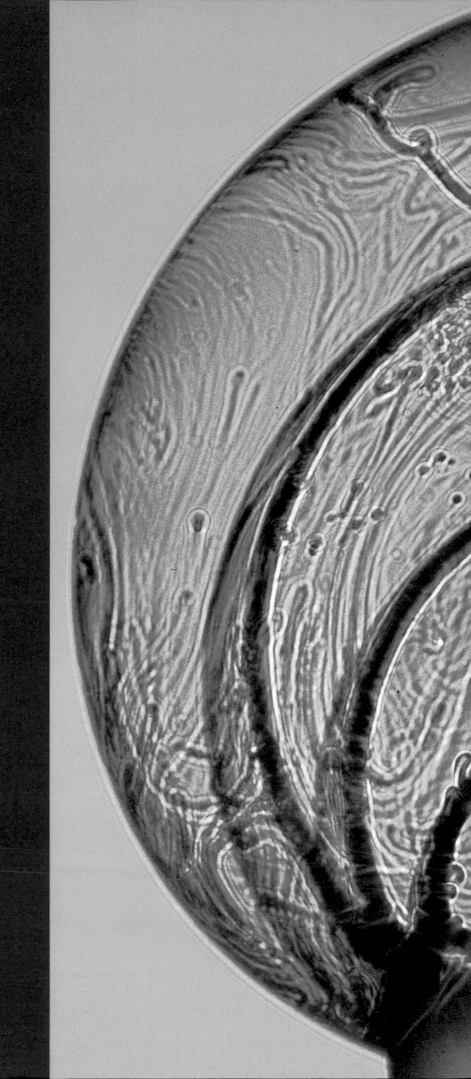

Lightweight Construction

## In the Beginning was the Bubble. Frei Otto Moves into New Construction Territory

A thin film, stretched over rods, rings and various models. This shimmering mixture of soap and water pointed the way to the best possible shape for technical membranes: the so-called minimal surface, with its ideal distribution of tension learned from nature. And something that had worked in small-scale experiments was destined to be successful on a large scale as well. Frei Otto wanted to open up new paths for architecture, using innovative cable-net structures, membranes and pneumatics. He applied the appropriate creativity to his models—and he was prepared to experiment. It didn't matter what was happening: membranes that opened out like krakens to protect visitors at open-air events, or pneumatic structures deriving their form entirely from air—the search for the best possible form was crucial to his design process. One point applicable to any conventional structure was crucial to Frei Otto's lightweights—they had to be calculated precisely if they were to stand up to wind and weather. His colleagues switched on their specially designed soap-film machine over and over again and made records of the fragile models it produced. These slide series have survived by the cupboardful. The architect worked as an engineer and a research scientist at Stuttgart's Institut für Leichte Flächentragwerke, IL for short, using the surface tension in soapsuds to study elemental form acquisition processes and then transfer them to the world of construction. Frei Otto was no longer content with the architect's traditional role. He linked different disciplines and questions together to gain new insights. He once said that the modern architect "has to adopt the best and the most suitable things, no matter where they may come from … he [has to] invent, experiment, develop and research for himself."[1] But the lightweight quality of his sensational structures was not achieved effortlessly. When Frei Otto published his magnum opus *Seifenblasen* (Soap Bubbles) in 1987, he and his teams had spent over 35 years with this special medium, and had developed these forms, some of which broke completely new ground "alone and without a model."[2] His uncompromising ethic, which required "genuinely new"[3] elements from every structure, shows how strongly innovation and construction are linked in Frei Otto's work, indeed that they are the engine behind it.

Innovation is Frei Otto's trademark. He was born in Siegmar (Saxony) on 31 May 1925, and is the embodiment of the path taken by a European inventor à la Buckminster Fuller.[4] Like Fuller he was working against the spirit of the times, but unlike the American, who was thirty years older, he soon found institutional support at college. He came from a family of sculptors, and became interested in model-making at an early stage. He was a pilot in the Second World War, and was commissioned in the Chartres prisoner-of-war camp to rebuild bridges—almost without any material. His gift for improvisation led him down completely new paths. As an architectural student at the Technical University in Berlin, Frei Otto took

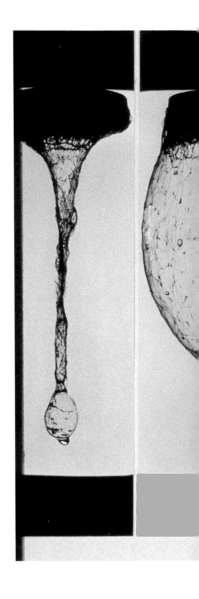

◄ From soap bubble to membrane: Frei Otto's experiments with bubbles illustrate ideal tension distribution for membranes. His legendary buildings would not have been possible without this systematic research.

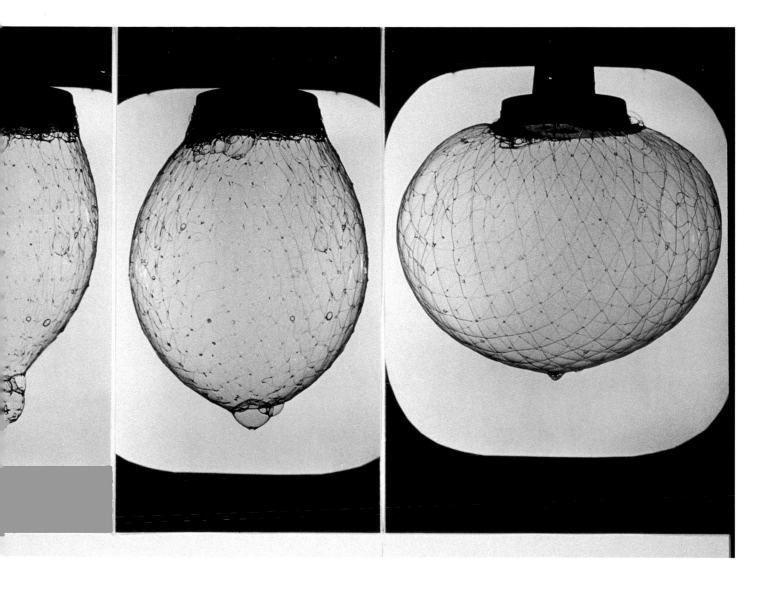

Testing to bursting-point: all the bubble experiments like this load-bearing test on a soap film were documented in detail and measured so that they could serve as a basis for actual buildings.

part in an exchange visit to the United States in 1950, studied at the University of Virginia and met Eero Saarinen and Fred Severud, who with Matthew Nowicki and William H. Deltrick were just planning the arena in Raleigh, North Carolina (1953–54). Their unusually light roof membrane, supported by steel cables suspended from two diagonally placed parabolic arches, inspired Otto. He was magically attracted to new constructional territory like this. As an architect with diploma he devoted himself to specialized construction forms that were hardly significant otherwise, and perfected pre-stressed cable-net systems, having by now gained his doctorate. In these suspended roofs, masses of crossed ropes are linked to surfaces that curve against each other to form a kind of net that is pre-stressed so that it will not lose its shape under changing loads.

The breakthrough from a peripheral existence involving élitist special structures to the centre of social discourse is marked by the 1967 Expo Pavilion in Montreal, designed with Rolf Gutbrod. Countering Buckminster Fuller' gigantic geodesic dome, which was intend to embrace the whole world symbolically, Frei Otto embarked on a much more modest

path, at least as far as dimensions were concerned.[5] His equal-mesh cable-net structure suspended on eight masts with its polyester fabric hanging underneath became an undulating landscape on the exhibition site. The membrane between the masts spanned 8,000 square metres, broken only by ellipsoid apertures to the sky. These let light into the pavilion and implemented something that Frei Otto had already tried out on soap films: gaps that form within a loop of rope if the film of soap, which is flat at first, is carefully drawn upwards.

Five years later—Otto's work had been given the accolade of an exhibition at the Museum of Modern Art (MoMA) in New York in 1971—he took the idea of the sensational Expo construction further, building the Olympic sports facilities in Munich with Günther Behnisch. In the 1967 competition model a ladies' nylon stocking had to stand in to show the spider's web structure of the roofs in three dimensions, but in the finished building this became an aesthetic and technological manifesto. At 34,500 square metres, the Olympic roof was over four times larger then the

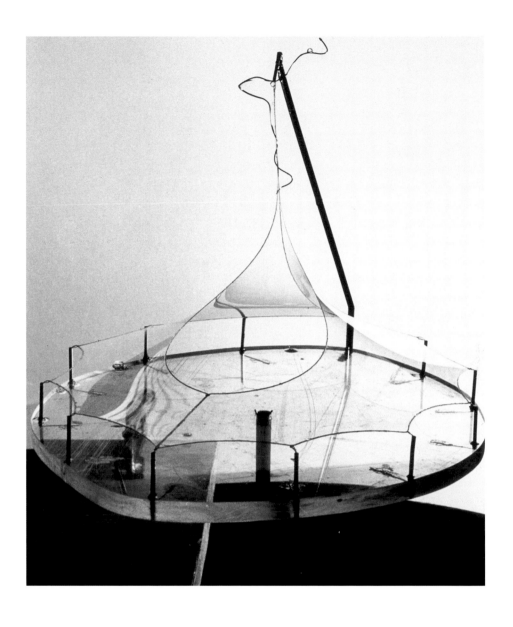

◄ High-wire act over 8,000 square metres of artificial landscape: fitters working on the 1967 Montreal Expo Pavilion between masts up to 38 metres high, until the lustrous membrane is stretched over the structure.

▶ Experiment and reality: model of the 1968 ILEK (Institute of Lightweight Structures) building in Vaihingen, Stuttgart and the building that was subsequently erected: the characteristic glazed eye in the 460 square metres of roof areas admits light into the body of the building.

pavilion in Montreal. The support structures were correspondingly large. Massive masts, cables and ground anchorage points[6] were needed to support the huge acrylic glass panes of the roof—a dozen anchored steel pylons that stabilized the roof as it soared into the sky. The Munich Olympic stadium was intended to symbolize a new, free Germany as organizer of these supposedly light-hearted games. But in terms of construction it became a pinnacle and a turning point in the history of cable-net structures. The massive anchoring system threatened to destroy the effect of the light roof, which offered a brilliant continuation of the landscape in the newly created Olympic park. The model using a jaunty women's stocking had solidified to become a steel and concrete monument.

A sensational thrust into new dimensions in its day: the 1972 Munich Olympic Stadium designed by Frei Otto with Günther Behnisch has a 34,000 square metre membrane above it.

Limits of growth: massive pylons, steel cables and anchoring points in the ground are needed to support the 22,000 square metres of roof over the Olympic Swimming Arena.

The bubble had burst. From then on, computers and calculation models used the finite element process to arrive at more rapid conclusions about form and the flow of forces in construction. The lightweight architect did not have to bother with soap bubble experiments any longer. His famous experimental machine is now a somewhat dusty presence in the building housing the Institut für Leichtbau, Entwerfen und Konstruieren (ILEK) that emerged from Frei Otto's research laboratory. The building itself, thrusting out like a spider's web, is overgrown with greenery. Frei Otto always warned against abusing nature as a stock of ideas for cheap copies, but nature seems to have detected that it is related to the research building and has snuggled up close to it. Inspired by the success of the Olympic roof, Frei Otto gained another mammoth contract in his homeland before finally launching his visions on the world market: the multi-purpose hall for the 1975 National Horticultural Show in Mannheim became the "culmination of his grid shell research and demonstrates the feasibility and economy of these compression structures at any scale."[7] The structure sat on the exhibition site like an enormous amoeba. Its lattice shell thrust into new dimensions: 72 kilometres of slats, fastened together by 38,000 bolts, a structure that could not have been calculated without the help of a computer and whose boldness is still reflected in Shigeru Ban's pavilion for Expo 2000, about which Frei Otto was consulted. The computer had not taken over completely.

Attack of the giant amoeba: Frei Otto developed a domed shell structure using 34,000 bolts and 72 kilometres of laths for the National Garden Show in Mannheim in 1975.

The interior of the grid shell in Mannheim opened up a new spatial experience—light and airy structures over corridors and passages. Shigeru Ban also decided on a comparable structure for his Expo 2000 Pavilion in Hanover.

Above the roofs of Stuttgart: openness, transparency and light are qualities distinguishing Werner Sobek's own R 128 house. The space opens up on to an incomparable view of the green valley.

An astonishing feature of a high-tech living machine like R 128: the individual floors are linked by traditional stairs. In the background is the free-standing bath-tub on the second floor.

◄ Werner Sobek designed one of the most unusual family homes of recent years. The cube consists only of glass and steel. It is the result of a technical and ecological experiment.

## The Next Generation. Werner Sobek's Art of Archi-neering and His R 128 House

"Secondary matters? I don't know what you're talking about!"[8] said Werner Sobek, who took over from Frei Otto at IL in 1995. He went on to say that our responsibility to society and the environment demands careful design, as each detail says something about the whole, and vice versa.[9] Ethics and design are inseparably linked for this architect-engineer. This applies to the formal and logical stringency of what is built as well as to its aesthetics, manageability and tactile qualities. As the new director of IL, he presided over its merger with another engineering department to become the present Institut für Leichtbau, Entwerfen und Konstruieren (ILEK). This is a unique institution, with engineers and architects working under the same roof on an equal footing. Like the pioneer of light plane load-bearing structures, his successor also has a vision with the potential to bring back together the two groups that have been drifting apart since the nineteenth century: the vision of a designed environment. Sobek calls for aesthetic care in designing anonymous artefacts like bridges, noise barriers and bus shelters. This mission is reminiscent of "good form" in the 1950s, but extends it into an ecological and pragmatic approach that has espoused the cause of transparency, modularity and recyclability. Sobek realized this trio above all in his own house, which has the model name R 128. The building is at 128 Römerstrasse—hence the name—and caused quite a stir in Stuttgart's well-ordered idyll: an uncompromising steel and glass cube, confidently placing itself within the history of Modernism and continuing it. Anyone looking at this glass and steel monolith will see an intelligent continuation of a tradition from Mies via Philip Johnson into the third millennium. A kind of version 2.0 of classical Modernism, combining transparency with high-tech sensors and user-menu controls to make a no-heat-energy building whose demolition was built into the design process. R 128 can be completely dismantled and recycled. Environmentally damaging combinations of materials that would have to be disposed of as hazardous waste are reduced to their structural core. Flexible electrical and sanitary installations permit almost any kind of modification to the inner life of the glass box, which certainly does quote Frei Otto's 1969 studio and home in Warmbronn, although the latter is not a dedicated eco-building. R 128, as the name suggests, is committed to technology. Ceilings with water flowing through them absorb solar energy in summer and take it via a heat exchanger to a long-term energy storage unit that emits it again in winter. The lightweight steel skeleton structure was worked out down to the last detail and assembled precisely, module by module. It simply could not be lighter. This house on a steep slope rests on a floor-slab without a cellar; its dimensions are the same as an earlier building, and so in many ways it is tailored to its location.

Sobek's ILEK Stuttgart is encouraging the connection between architecture and engineering in the hope that something new will come out of their crossing each other's borders, engineering that will emancipate itself from the role of executive specialist planner or architect's fulfilment aid—in favour of interactive co-operation with the other in each case. Sobek has set an example in his years of teamwork with Helmut Jahn. Jahn calls this "archi-neering,"[10] and its has made an impact so far particularly in case of the Sony-Center in Berlin and Bangkok airport. In the latter project, an elevated canopy 40 metres above ground level and almost 1,000 metres long had to be developed, under which the actual airport terminal had to seem as "immaterial" as possible, completely glazed and "supported only by a few cable braces."[11] This simple guideline led to an intensive exchange between architect and engineer. Sobek remembers that details were developed in Stuttgart, to some extent "quite naturally, on the telephone."[12] Sobek actually feels that there is not really a name for his profession: "Structural engineer fits to an extent, and I am not an architect in the usual sense; I am a bit more like an ordinary engineer."[13] Despite the fact that he crosses a number of boundaries, Sobek certainly is one thing: a perfectionist. For this Swabian born in 1953, engineering should be a statement about how the world should function. He says that there is something that holds this world together in a most profound way—and on this point he sounds almost Faustian—and that this has an effect on the form of architecture, which does not just serve as an envelope, but as the most important part of our world, as a manifestation of our society.[14]

Sobek campaigns for maximum architectural performance using minimal quantities of materials and the greatest possible degree of environmental friendliness. And so he does not rely solely on standard solutions from architectural history like frames, girders and arches, but poaches from areas that are sometimes quite distant, like car manufacture and aircraft construction. The design process evolves more by analogy with car safety technology processes and with evolution. When designing load-bearing structures, Sobek tries to structure the forces in the space and to supply the channels of force produced in this way with "materials that are suitable for pressure or tensile loading."[15] Sobek acquired knowledge about textiles and how to cut them for mobile protective roofs whose membranes can cover the arenas in Nîmes or Zaragoza in the shortest possible time. One of his most beautiful innovations goes back to this. It is tiny by comparison—a model on the table—and at the same time succinct: sunshades that manage completely without ribs and are stabilized exclusively by centrifugal force. You press a button and the slack strips of material start to turn, fill out and rise, until they reach their full height and unfurl to their full extent. The idea dates from 1997; the execution was considerably more complex, as account had to be taken both of the aerodynamics of the umbrellas as they unfold like bells, their span and the weight of the fabric, and also the revs of the motor accommodated in the mast.

Small model, big impact: Werner Sobek's umbrellas spin round their own axes at the touch of a button and open themselves as a result of centrifugal force. They do not require either ribs or mechanical parts.

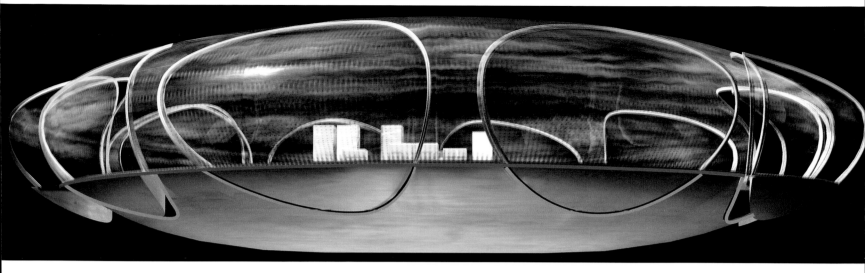

A UFO from the computer: the R 129 circular structure and technology depot is in the tradition of Buckminster Fuller's spectacular Witchita House, though it is equipped with all the luxury of the 21st century.

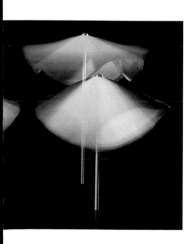

## Building R 129: the High-Tech Ark

The experimental structure called R 129, which follows R 128 only in name, offers prospects for the future. This technical device developed by Werner Sobek and Maren Sostmann can be recycled and is durable, and also completely self-sufficient. The computer study is intended to anticipate developments. In fact R 129 looks like a an alien artefact in the otherwise rigid world of building. Like Buckminster Fuller's Witchita House it breaks with the way a house is expected to look: the plastic envelope of the lenticular spheroid became an intelligent membrane, coated on the outside with a layer of glass one millimetre thick, which is scratch- and chemical-resistant, and solar cells, which again provide the majority of the building's energy supply. The metal-evaporated envelope prevents heat radiation inwards (in summer) or outwards (in winter). Electrochromous foil makes it possible for the transparent envelope to become opaque if wished. The building's interior life is as spectacular as the exterior is unconventional: a fluid spatial continuum reminiscent of the pneumatic world of the 1960s and provided with sanitary and kitchen installations from a movable central unit containing the facilities. The carbon-body floor slab has heating and cooling systems built into it, and also contains the mechanical ground ventilation system with heat recovery and optional water treatment. The description of the building says that R 129 offers the chance of living "in the closest possible contact with nature, with a very high degree of comfort … The building envelope is almost completely dematerialized, which blurs the boundaries between inside and outside, providing a fluent transition from the living space to the sky."[16] And so a modern ark has been produced, with utopian elements like fabrics that can change colour, glass with adjustable transmission and load-changing building components.[17] It attempts a symbiosis with nature—as a dream of a new technosphere, reconciling the built world and the environment.

Membranes and Light Materials

## The Mother of All Tents. Richard Rogers' Millennium Dome in London

This was where the new millennium was due to begin. Right on the Greenwich meridian, "time's official home," at least since 1884. Popping champagne corks and three cheers for the Queen. But it wasn't the venerable Old Royal Observatory that was at the centre of things, but an industrial site a mile or two downstream. This is where the masses were to come flooding, to a place that had only attracted scouts looking for cheap building land for years, to the Millennium Dome, which lords it over south-east London like a gigantic UFO. This thing from another world has the world's largest Teflon roof. Old master Sir Richard Rogers suspended it from twelve 100-metre-high masts and 70 kilometres of cable. Pure white, and gleaming, in a way that architecture had not done since the International Style. Fifty metres high at its apex, 320 metres in diameter, a gigantic volume that still had to be filled. A manifesto for lightness, with room for 18,000 red double-decker buses and a domed roof that could swallow Wembley stadium twice over. The mother of all tents was swamped by figures and records right up to its opening day. An area of 200,000 square metres and 80,000 square metres of membrane—PTFE-coated fibreglass—an absolutely masterly achievement, in terms of the speed with which the structure was erected as well. The first piles were rammed into the bankside silt on 23 June 1997, with no one suspecting that this was industrial wasteland. The masts were in position by October. The cables took their load in March 1998. The multi-layered

Body Zone, an installation by Doug Branson and Nigel Coates inside the Millennium Dome, welcomed the visitors.

▶ A technical miracle of statics and engineering, but now just a beautiful envelope without a function on industrial wasteland.

◀ Richard Rogers' Millennium Dome in London is the largest tented structure in the world and dominates the banks of the nearby Thames. It is 320 metres in diameter, with almost 80,000 square metres of Teflon-coated glass fibre membrane spanning a dozen masts to form a gleaming white circle on the east side of the city.

roof should shine out over London for 25 years, and engineers said that the masts would last for 60 years. It will probably not come to this. Even though the adventure cost just less than 1,024 million pounds in state and lottery money. Another 359 million pounds were to be raised through admission tickets, sponsorship and merchandising. As things have turned out, this was a gigantic illusion. The powers that be had tried everything. The Queen and Prime Minister Tony Blair were as relaxed as protocol allowed at the opening, and even James Bond clambered around the matt white Teflon roof. A massive marketing and media campaign was unleashed, and it is easy to gain the impression that there were so many side events that the actual star of the show was forgotten: the Millennium Dome as a technical miracle of its day, like Joseph Paxton's Crystal Palace about 150 years before.

If there had not been a few ambitious pavilions, truly lightweight structures, the whole affair could have been forgotten. The attractions were laid out in a circle around a central arena. They offered a fair of competing vanities, with star architects like Nigel Coates and Zaha Hadid appearing to transform themes like "body" or "mind" into architecture. Coates' Body Zone was immediately adjacent to the main entrance, a couple locked in an intimate embrace, fused into a larger-than-life-size sculpture, and marking out one creative approach. Zaha Hadid's constructive high-tech was diametrically opposed to this. Her Mind Zone towered straight up to tent heaven in the form of a gigantic ramp. Visitors could relax in a chill-out zone designed by Richard Rogers, probably as a contemptuous compensation for the fact that the noble dimensions of his dome had been vitiated by dozens of insertions. Today the millennium experiment is long past, and nobody knows what the dome's future will be. In early 2003 there was news of a new scheme coming up for Greenwhich peninsula—10,000 homes, shops, a school and a hotel. The dome will be turned into an entertainment and sports arena for more than 26,000 spectators—similar to its much smaller US-counterparts.

## Membranes Over Plush. Klaus Latuske's Musical Theatre in Hamburg for The Lion King

Night over Hamburg, blue and inky-dark. The harbour—a sea of light. Opposite the St Pauli landing stages, where the Hanseatic city seems even more maritime, there is a structure glowing out towards the centre in an almost challenging yellow: the musical theatre for Disney's *The Lion King*. Klaus Latuske designed the arched hall as a transportable theatre for *Buddy—the Musical* in 1994. As this exotic presence on the site of the former Stülken shipyard was to be demolished after a mere two years, each of the five trusses could be taken apart into five pieces, and snap bolts in the foundations meant that the mobile theatre really could go on tour. Five steel braced arches spanned 55 metres, five times 25 tons of steel arched over the audience, forming a column-free space with an unimpeded view of the stage. Latuske was not just trying to package expensive stage technology aesthetically, he wanted to make the 1,400-strong audience comfortable as well. Protected by an air-space up to 30 centimetres wide between the membranes to absorb noise and weather, the musical-lovers sat in plush seats, relaxed, and enjoyed the show. No wonder the mobile theatre felt more like a lavish hall than a big top. This was due to the effortless span of the arch trusses—there was room for stage, seating, foyer and restaurant under something like a gigantic umbrella. Faced with this perfection, it is no wonder that the musical the-atre remained standing and even survived its first show. But everything changed in spring 1991: it only took eight months to convert the light-weight theatre covered in its multi-layered membrane completely—and to stop it moving. The mobile tent became a proper theatre building. Every-thing under the massive steel structure was renewed: an understage and a 25 metre high fly tower were added. An additional balcony raised the maxi-mum audience capacity to 1926 seats. A five-storey management building went up next to the stage, auditorium and foyer, and also a restaurant and a ferry landing-pier with direct access to the foyer. It was finished by 30 November 2001—although it was scarcely discernible from the outside, the lightweight theatre covered by a multi-layered membrane had put on many pounds. As before, the yellow membrane was stretched across the sup-ports, which were held on both sides by six paired steel cables. Now the mobile theatre was fixed, and the *The Lion King* could begin.

Klaus Latuske's tent for the musical *The Lion King* makes no secret of its origins. The mem-brane structure was originally intended to remain mobile, but the theatre in Hamburg harbour was made permanent in 2001.

Klaus Latuske

The taut membrane is as weather-proof as a solid roof. It protects the structure below it in several layers.

The five welded steel lattice arches above the musical tent span 55 metres. This structure gives the set designers new creative freedom in the interior and provides an open view of the stage for spectators.

## Two Extraordinary Travelling Exhibition Buildings. Andreas Heller's LiebesLeben and SehnSucht

Andreas Heller specializes in polished interiors and trade show presentations, and he wants to get "right up close"[1] to what's happening. His Hamburg design studio has produced two transportable exhibition structures: LiebesLeben (LoveLife) and SehnSucht (Longing). Liebes-Leben has been touring for the Cologne Federal Central Health Education office since 1994. The pavilion with its 260 square metres of exhibition space concentrates on an urgent topic: AIDS prevention. For this reason Heller did not create a neutral envelope or a container for any old thing, but a compact pavilion, highly symbolic in character—in the shape of a heart. "We wanted to be at the very centre of the cities whatever happened," Heller emphasized, "so that quite normal adults will feel like coming in."[2] The tarpaulin-covered aluminium structure had to be appropriately light. The approach paid off: on average there were 2,500 visitors per day, as many as 7,000 in Frankfurt. The structure has now been erected and dismantled dozens of times. The crew do not even need a screwdriver or a spanner to assemble their pavilion, which looks like a sunken heart, as it is held together by stainless steel bolts. "The trick is imagining how the

The LiebesLeben exhibition pavilion does not look out of place in a good middle-class background, as here in Bonn. It is not too high, and thus all the more elegant, and can effortlessly stand in the middle of a square without dominating it.

Inside a surprisingly lavish area of exhibition space is revealed, so that visitors can look at the exhibits in peace. There is even room for a flight of steps.

assembly team really work, which hand is free,"[3] says Heller, as in his opinion that is the only way to save time . On average, LiebesLeben can be put up in one and a half days.

Two years later, in 1996, the SehnSucht exhibition set off on tour. Heller benefited from his experience with LiebesLeben, even though the exhibition space required was almost double—400 square metres. Once again the designers made the connections as simple as possible, but the increased size did come at a price. This structure takes five days to assemble or dismantle. Nothing changed in the basic principle. The transportable building again consists of two lorry trailers that are used as a cinema and a lounge respectively during the exhibition, again the load-bearing structure is in aluminium, and a water container is used for stabilization purposes. What attracts Heller to ephemeral structures? He doesn't need to think very long about that: playing with the moment, the apparently "unserious" or even "careless"[4] quality of a design for a few weeks only. And of course the hints of moving accommodation for showpeople, travellers and other attractions. Transportable buildings accompany new entertainment forms and go back to archaic ideas to do so, tarpaulins and masts, but of course without looking as though they are only temporary.

Andreas Heller's larger SehnSucht exhibition pavilion offers 400 travelling square metres. The aluminium support structure and water-tank can be loaded on to lorries in a few days and transported to the next venue.

The contrast could not be greater, and that is its charm. The eternal and the ephemeral—SehnSucht outside Cologne Cathedral.

Benno Bauer's culture centre in Puchheim, Munich seems quite free of care. There is no outward sign of the complexities of the Teflon membrane as the provider of heat and noise insulation, nor of the elaborate structure needed for the eight pairs of timber trusses.

## Surfing the Wave. Benno Bauer's Culture Centre in Puchheim, Munich

This is a building that is quite different. It looks very solid from the street, towering towards the park in a dramatic gesture, like a wave in the surf shortly before it crashes down on the gravel. The white membrane roof of the Puchheim culture centre, with an area of almost 1,000 square metres, caused quite a stir. The dormitory town just outside Munich wanted to use it to brighten up its image—and went for advanced architecture. Benno Bauer cunningly chose a conventional entrance, rectangular, solid and almost inconspicuous. Toughened with reinforced concrete, the mandatory approach, as it were. The architect did his own thing with the events hall for 800 people, a light-weight structure made up of steel girders, wooden arch frames and a

A pleasantly close relationship with the people: Benno Bauer won the International Textile Architecture Prize for this unusual culture centre in 1999.

Teflon roof. Eight separate pairs of trusses form a ribbed vault that is supported by the reinforced concrete ceiling of the entrance building and then by light hinged columns. Bauer was awarded the 1999 International Textile Architecture Prize for this constructional masterpiece. The dynamic envelope rapidly became the culture centre's visual trademark. Bauer is an analyst who leaves nothing to chance: "A structural section using the differential construction method consists of several elements that are

comparatively simple as such,"[5] is Bauer's comment on the membrane roof, which required an optimization of the structure before it could be constructed. The architect decided on a multi-layered model. The outer and inner membranes are made of non-combustible textile fabric. They were coated with PVC to make them water-resistant. Insulation and a vapour barrier were followed by a fabric strip that can absorb over 50 decibels. This means that each square metre of roof produces a load of 20 kilograms, almost two tons all together. These forces are braced by a mass of cables stabilizing the eight pairs of trusses. From the outside they show up as elegant ribs against the immaculately white membrane. The building seems light and lively, without giving a hint of the structural effort behind it. Bauer taught at the Stuttgart Institut für Leichtbau, Entwerfen und Konstruieren (ILEK) for a long time. This meant that specialists—structural engineers, thermodynamics and acoustics experts—were always on hand to meet the high level of requirements relating to noise, heat and fire protection in a public place. "Every building remains a prototype,"[6] says Bauer, alluding to early achievements using lightweight engineering techniques like the Zeppelin. And so it is very comforting to know that the Teflon envelope is barely flammable.

Stretched textile fabrics make the interior design both light and spacious. And they conceal everything that does not fit in with their elegant curves: only the trusses are visible.

Inflatable Architecture

## There's Something in the Air. Axel Thallemer's Airtecture and Airquarium

The inflatable structure revolution meant negotiating corners: Airtecture, a musclebound, yet highly sensitive, indeed intelligent structure that responded directly to wind and weather. Its originator, Axel Thallemer, made a radical break from the idea that pneumatic structures had to be round in the mid 1990s. In 1996, Airtecture offered a completely new spatial experience in the Swabian town of Esslingen, the home of Festo AG & Co—it was as rectangular and sturdy as a normal building. Without the usual airlocks and typical hissing sounds as you go in. This sounds quite normal, but Airtecture in fact looks pretty dramatic. Two rows of Y-columns flank the actual hall like a guard of honour—energetic and muscular. You enter Airtecture as a naturally ventilated and lit hall that seems both strange and familiar. A long space opens up, 375 square metres in area, with walls six metres high, alternately translucent and completely opaque. Light—dark—light—dark, zebra stripes, there to take away the feeling of weight and load. Even the ceiling seems to dissolve in the rhythmically alternating bands of light. There is a great deal of innovative power behind the extraordinary aesthetics of this exhibition hall, which won the prestigious Industrial Design Award in 1997. When all is said and done, Airtecture is the first building in the world with a rectangular interior whose load-bearing structure is largely based on air chambers. A load-bearing structure made up of 40 Y-columns stabilizes the central cubic box; their active pneumatic elements respond directly to changing wind loads, rain and snow. The polyamide fabric with an inner silicon tube, which actually is called "muscle," can be regulated variably to respond to load transfer. About 330 computer-controlled units react to storm or calm by changing the internal pressure and the volume. To do this, the requirements stored in the computer memory are matched to actual values from the in-house weather station, and translated into tension or

◄ Axel Thallemer's Airquarium is heated from below by warm air admitted through thermostatically controlled air vents. Used air then escapes through the ventilator in the middle of the dome. This achieves optimum heat and ventilation control.

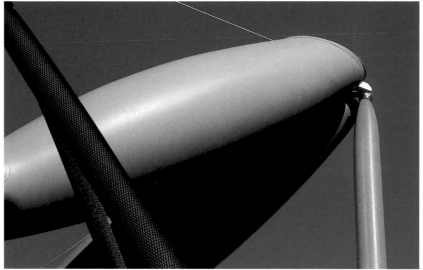

Ambiguous and angular: Axel Thallemer opened up new dimensions for building with air with his Airtecture hall, designed for Festo. He produced an apparently conventional rectangular hall, without the usual curves associated with pneumatic buildings. Daylight is admitted through translucent areas running round the long sides and the hall ceiling like stripes.

Airtecture's pairs of side supports are airship-taut. They respond actively to changing wind and snow loads by relaxing or tightening their pneumatic "muscles."

Airtecture's secret lies in its cleverly devised structure consisting of air-filled beams on the roof and Y-shaped supports flanking the building and holding it up.

relaxation. The expressive play of muscles on the sides of the building is balanced by the reticence of the 36 dual-wall elements that make up the walls, straight runs of spacer fabric operating at a working pressure of 0.5 bars to form the walls of the hall with its volume of 2,250 cubic metres. The roof in its turn is loosely reinforced by alternating airbeams—inflated chambers—carrying positive pressure and transparent membrane sections carrying negative pressure. And so the aesthetic effect of the play of light and shade inside is based on a structural solution—an amazing insight. Axel Thallemer has used enormous finesse to remove any sense of being temporary from inflatable structures, replacing gentle curves with a mechanical ballet of pneumatic muscles and computer-controlled regulation techniques. Even though the structure comes in at an airy seven and a half kilograms per square metre, Airtecture weighs a total of six tons that can be accommodated in a 12-metre container. But as soon as the hall moves to a new location it needs regular foundations. Ultimately the structure offers 5,760 cubic metres of building volume on a base area of 800 square metres. The fact that, four years after Airtecture, Thallemer took the classical inflatable hall to its limits with Airquarium confirms the value of the development rather than suggesting a contradiction. Ultimately Thallemer's credo is this: "The designer has to question all processes fundamentally, not just the formal ones."[1]

Like water, you think involuntarily, gossamer-thin, as you stroke the transparent fabric with its bluish shimmer. The Vitroflex envelope feels smooth and at the same time pleasantly tensioned. There is no sign of foundations or supports. This eight metre high plastic sphere is supported by nothing but air. Its skin curves firmly upwards to the apex. The whole thing is stabilized by a ring filled with water. Water and air—the two images start to run together, becoming as transparent as the membrane that the inflatable structure is made of. This impression is deliberate: Thallemer's

The Airquarium is 32 metres in diameter and eight metres high, which provides enough space for a neat little touring exhibition. Water can be introduced into a tubular ballast tank running right round the Airquarium to stabilize the structure. When folded up, it fits into a single 12-metre container.

Strange but true: classic cars, for example, look good here—but there are 800 square metres available anyway. The hall's rotunda shape means that visitors have no difficulty in finding their way about.

so-called Airquarium, dating from the year 2000, links the two elements and adds them to the canon of building materials as though they were wood or stone. And even more: they become catalysts for pure design in which construction and envelope—the building's skin and bones—became as one. It is no accident that this perfect hemisphere is like a bubble, evenly diverting the load downwards via the tensioned membrane. The inflatable structure supports itself entirely on high air pressure in the interior, and then the structure, which has no foundations, is stablized by water. To do this, circular tanks around the base take 120 tons of ballast water (120,000 litres), enough to resist all the wind loads that buffet the domed hall. A brilliant idea. Unlike concrete piles and walls, water is available in almost unlimited quantities and can be pumped in and out again without difficulty. A strange idea: set up, pump up, fill up and stick the services on—the Airquarium is ready for use, as a mobile exhibition and events hall. Procedures that seem more like starting to use a familiar apparatus than a real piece of architecture. This mobile air and water bubble with its handsome diameter of 32 metres and a height of eight metres seems to be stressed to bursting-point. Anyone who wants to get inside the hemisphere has to get through two airlocks. This is not fussy security, not intended to harass, but a structural necessity. Without the double airlock the Airquarium would collapse like a balloon envelope whose burner has failed. As in all inflatable structures, you have a sense of the airflow, or rather you hear it: a slight light buzzing sound is audible as soon as you have got past the first door. Air flows sideways past you, positive pressure that keeps the hall in shape. After a few steps over an aluminium floor you come to the second airlock, the one that actually leads into the interior. Then an immaculate dome soars up, weightless, simple and beautiful, rising eight metres towards the sky. Light floods into the interior, and the surroundings show through the membrane as though it were a piece of greaseproof paper. Clouds pass across this great canvas, slightly milky but clearly recognizable, things seem to be both a long way off and very close. The structure changes its pressure according to the wind load, pumps itself up a bit more or slackens off. Despite its scale the Airquairium is still a large mobile structure that can be transported comfortably in two containers. The services—air conditioning, fan, heating and water-changer for cooling—are provided by an emergency generator unit and are thus independent of location.

## Cool Britannia. Doug Branson's and Nigel Coates' Powerhouse::UK

The revolution of the 1990s was in the name of achieving perfection. Shedding all the ideological ballast of the 1960s, which celebrated this kind of light and temporary structure as the dawn of a new society, today's structures seem like an everyday update of what were then revolutionary utopias. What had happened? A new generation of artists and designers set about being creative without any prejudice or barriers. Two of these are Doug Branson and Nigel Coates, whose Powerhouse::UK pavilion became the star of the Horse Guards Parade exhibition in London in 1998, a show intended to present British creativity in the fields of learning, networking, communication and lifestyle. Everything fitted perfectly. The pavilion's four air-cushion drums, arranged like clover leaves and lit in bluish light, suddenly seemed like the quintessence of everything that the fresh and youthful Prime Minister Tony Blair had proclaimed—"Cool Britannia" had found a suitable symbol. The commission for Powerhouse::UK was placed in September 1997, as a result of a competition run by the British Department of Trade and Industry. The aim was to embody Great Britain's creative strengths—a symbolic structure for the ASAM II Asia summit, which was ultimately open to all Londoners as well as to delegates from the Far East. Instead of developing a pure inflatable structure, Branson and Coates decided for safety reasons

Doug Branson and Nigel Coates designed the Powerhouse::UK pavilion in 1998. Four red carpets led from the information stand in the central lobby towards the four silver-foil space capsules that make up the exhibition building.

Modern Nomads

Recycling in its most beautiful form: the pavilion was 72 metres long and 25 metres wide. It was made of cardboard tubes and wooden laths, covered with a paper membrane and weather-proof sheeting. It was not just a feast for the eye, it could be dismantled and completely recycled.

◄ A building that is not of this world: the undulating cardboard roof of Shigeru Ban's Japanese Pavilion made it the greatest draw for the public at Expo 2000 in Hanover.

## Temporary Buildings for All Seasons. Shigeru Ban's Curtain Wall House in Tokyo, His Expo 2000 Pavilion in Hanover and His Emergency Accommodation for Kobe

Wind stirs the white curtain. The fabric billows out against the angular corner of the building that thrusts out of the space like an arrow. Open storeys, open views. Shigeru Ban has mercilessly exposed intimate living and turned it outwards. An entire wall seems to have been replaced by fabric. If this were not down-town Tokyo you might well think of a villa by the sea and starched linen stirred by the breeze. Admittedly the architect had something else in mind. He had a vision of freedom, radical liberation from current housing con-cepts, from cocooning in the heart of our cities. Shigeru Ban's architecture tries to dissolve itself. Walls become permeable membranes with the out-side world, recycled rolls of paper or a curtain façade that takes the Mod-ernist invention of a glass wall between inside and outside literally and breaks it ironically. Living as a permanent experiment made Shigeru Ban's name, and he is systematically testing the boundaries, centimetre by centimetre, and then he opens up a new field with a sudden change of material, as in his 1995 Curtain Wall House.

Ban, who was born in 1957, may have asked himself "why have walls at all?" when he formulated his response to Mies van der Rohe's concept of fluid space with his Wall-less House in the Nagano prefecture in 1997. Japanese subtlety allows the walls to be simply pushed away, until all that is still standing under the flat roof are three delicate columns that are suddenly placed in an almost crazily distorted relationship to the open space under the massively protruding roof. The house opens up to the world completely, an elaborate experiment in living.

Shigeru Ban became famous at the latest for his Japanese Pavilion at Expo 2000 in Hanover. The world's largest paper and cardboard build-ing, 89 metres long, 42 metres wide and 16 metres high, suddenly became one of the main Expo attractions. Queues at the entrance and waiting times of half an hour were quite common if you wanted to go into this miracle consisting of 40 metre long cardboard tubes, interwoven to form a dynamic vault 16 metres above the visitors. "I had a feeling they were there as a net to catch us," was the enthusiastic response from one woman visitor to the pavilion. The lattice made up of 440 rolls precisely 12 centimetres in diameter was covered with a special fire- and water-proof paper membrane so that light could come in between the rolls—which made a crucial contribution to the spatial impression provided by the hall's rhythmic expansion and contraction. Shigeru Ban had conceived the undulating barrel shell in recycled paper with old master Frei Otto in such a way that it could be completely demolished and recycled after the Expo.

The spectacular success of the Expo building distracted attention from the fact that Shigeru Ban had already planned cardboard emergency accommodation and actually constructed it on behalf of the UN High

Shigeru Ban's Paperlog Houses were first used for victims of the Kobe earthquake in 1995. They provide emergency accommodation that can be set up at short notice and without a great deal of effort and expense. Their foundations are made up of empty beer crates stabilized with sandbags.

There is space in the smallest hut, as can be seen from this view of the inside of the emergency accommodation. The walls seem solid and reliable, the translucent ceiling gives a sense of relative spaciousness that cuts against the size constraints imposed.

Commission for refugees in Rwanda and elsewhere. Fifty prototypes were tested in 1998, shelters made of simple cardboard tubes that had to be able to stand up to termites in particular. Prefabricated plastic connections made them wonderfully simple to erect: put them together—tarpaulin on the top—ready. Ban had used a related principle after the devastating Kobe earthquake in 1995. Emergency hut accommodation was created on foundations made of worn-out beer crates filled with sand. These were easy to build and also reliably insulated against wind and weather, in summer and in winter. Ban used a structure of vertical cardboard tubes (diameter 10.8 centimetres), material that cost no more than 2,000 euros per hut. The aesthetic aspect was never neglected. "Refugee shelter has to be beautiful," Ban stressed, as "psychologically, refugees are damaged. They have to stay in nice places."[1] In Japan, with its long tradition of paper architecture, even an innovator like Ban cannot drop below standard.

Shigeru Ban's Curtain Wall House in Nagano achieved instant iconic status as soon as it was built in 1995. Concrete pillars take up the concept of floating, white Modernism, but billowing curtains make fun of the curtain-wall usually made of steel and glass.

Shigeru Ban

## Mobile Community Centre in No-Man's Land. Florian Nagler's Bürgerhaus in Neuperlach, Munich

Anyone who wants to follow Modernism's remorseless ageing process does not have to go to New York or Tokyo. It is enough to make a detour into the suburbs of any large town. That period has left its marks behind in Hanns-Seidl-Platz in the Munich district of Neuperlach. Unlovely high-rise apartment blocks, lifeless glass barrels and brick-armoured shopping fortresses stand noisily together as if in a bazaar. Heavy façades ruin the view, buildings that seem to be competing with each other to see which is the most trivial. And then there is something else: a newcomer has established itself opposite the weathered post-office pavilion, and it looks very different: flat and shed roof, protruding canopy, slender columns and clear forms—Florian Nagler's Bürgerhaus offers a brilliant counter-design to the ostentatious architecture around it.

Neuperlach has started to catch up on its urbanization with a temporary building. The 773 square metre pavilion intended to accommodate events is a ray of hope among the shopping malls, built in late autumn

A solid look despite its mobility: Florian Nagler's community centre in Neuperlach, Munich, was planned as a temporary building from the outset. But its finish makes it an absolute classic: it would be wonderful if it could stay here for a little longer.

Full marks for prefabrication. Walls were delivered as segments and could be assembled on site in a minimum of time.

A wonderful transition from closed to open space. Glass walls and a veranda give the community centre a relaxed and spacious quality that public buildings seldom achieve.

2001. The Bürgerhaus is made up of prefabricated container elements, and grew into a substantial 30 by 30 metre square, and its broad glass façade and doors are now inviting the citizens of Neuperlach in. The concept is as simple as it is brilliant. In the centre is the events hall, screened off by solid walls, around it are the offices, the kitchen and the Internet café. The auditorium holds 200 visitors, and if the ceiling-high doors to the foyer are opened it can easily become 300. The heavy doors disappear into the wall cavities between two container elements and create an increasingly large space, extending out under the canopy and further across Hanns-Seidl-Platz. Could there be a more welcoming gesture?

Many things about the structure seem paradoxical: it was intended to be temporary, and yet it radiates solidity, standing on the edge of the square and calming the excited, stagey architecture around it with its clear lines. There is a sense of impermanence around the Bürgerhaus, with its emphatically simple materials—USB slabs, plastic floors—and its spartan furnishings. But it does not seem cheap, quite the contrary. The strict rhythm of its prefabricated elements gives it unity and formal strength. From its show side, which gives a fleeting impression of Mies's National-galerie in Berlin when seen out of the corner of one's eye, to the emergency exit at the back everything seems to form an integrated whole. Inside, the light, which falls evenly and dazzle-free through a polycarbonate ceiling, enhances the quality of the space. Munich-based architect Florian Nagler left nothing to chance. But even though it has only just been erected, time is running out for the building. In four or five years' time it will have to give way and make room for the permanent community and culture centre. But who knows, temporary solutions often last for a very long time.

## More Than a Container. Matthias Loebermann's Infobox in Nuremberg

"I am interested in boundaries,"[2] Matthias Loebermann explains, meaning above all: breaking down conventions. Loebermann practises as an architect in Nuremberg and is professor at the Fachhochschule in Biberach. He regularly visits aerospace, shipping and textile trade shows, and thus becomes a commuter across boundaries. His experimental Infobox, which he simply calls a "built sketch,"[3] demonstrates his ideas on building with new, light and unconventional materials. Loebermann designed a pavilion that was driven on a low-loader to its chosen location in the form of a steel frame. Until 2000 this district information centre stood behind the mass of railway facilities relating to Nuremberg's main station, towering up like a town fortress in Celtisplatz. Its setting was a miserable strip of green called South Park and a disused strip of road. Not dream surroundings, but they do make it possible for advanced architecture to stand out very effectively. As if to make this clear, the pavilion floats above the ground on 16 individual cylindrical foundations—a homage to Modernism and a declaration of war against the no man's land in which it stands.

The information pavilion does not offer much more floor space than an average apartment: about 400 square metres. Of these, three quarters make up the exhibition space with its adjustable walls, and another 12 square metres provide a special exhibition area that can be divided off, the

The façade design of Matthias Loebermann's Infobox, which was in place in Nuremberg until 2000, combines simplicity and sophistication. This mobile structure seems to float lightly above the ground.

glass box. The remainder provides offices and sanitary facilities. Ultra-light materials are everywhere, from the cellulose-based, transparent heat insulation, usually found in aircraft fuselages, to the light-ceiling. Tiny, diagonally-cut acrylic glass tubes provide perfect light—as in a museum, just very much more cheaply. The entire glass box oscillates between exhibitionistic openness and private reticence. Loebermann's intention was to take a theme—transparency—and lay it open to sensual experience. He succeeded. Various systems—perforated aluminium panels, slats and translucent glass panels providing a high level of heat insulation—are juxtaposed. And they show how the quality of the space and its light can change. The pavilion had fulfilled its purpose by autumn 2000. The box was simply heaved on to a lorry and driven away. The primary school in Kornburg has used it as a pupils' common room ever since. It could have been worse.

For the turn of the millennium, Loebermann developed a completely different, mobile version of his exhibition system, the "RID Pavilion,"[4] intended to be assembled in three days. The solution was as simple as it was brilliant: scissor-shaped steel tubes extend continuously like a concertina until the basket-shell structure covers an area of 10 by 38 metres. But for transport by articulated lorry the pavilion shrinks to a compact package only three metres long, weighing only six tons, with an additional 600 kilograms of composite slabs as a floor covering. It could hardly be more compact, despite a ridge height of 5.5 metres.

Light in, sun out. Slats (right) and sliding wire grilles (left) give the façade a varied dynamic and change both the outward appearance and the interior effect in no time.

Whether the space is being used
for a conference, a gathering round
a table or an exhibition—if the room
dividers are not needed they look
good fastened back against the
wall.

Matthias Loebermann's aim was
the greatest possible flexibility,
inside and outside. Mobile screens
divide the pavilion into suitable
zones for various activities.

113  Matthias Loebermann

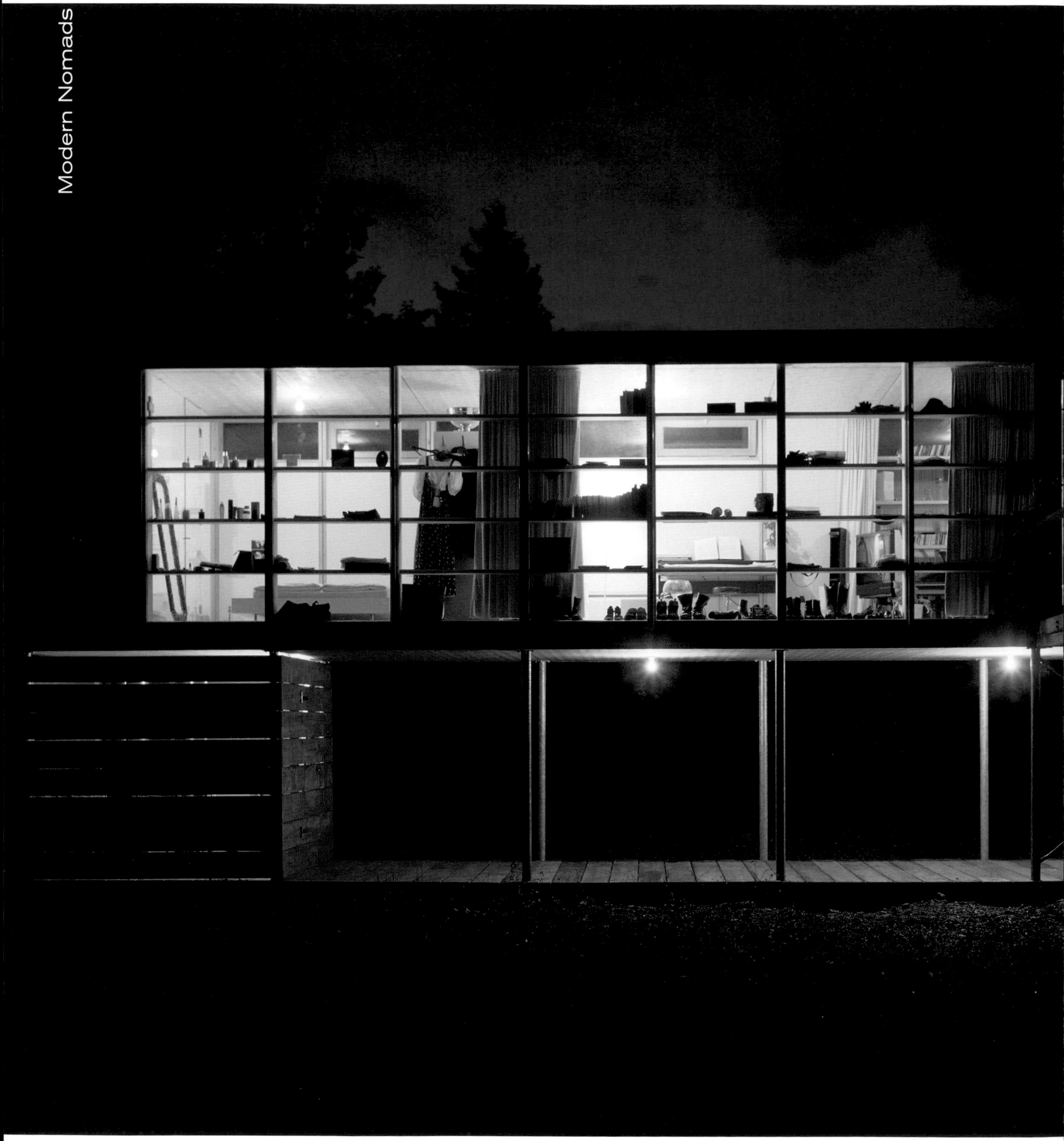

The beauty and lightness of Johannes Kaufmann's unusual Su-Si house make their greatest impact at night: a friendly and inviting interior. And he even remembered a carport.

Su-Si on its travels. At first glance you could mistake the house on wheels for a posh circus caravan on the move. But Su-Si does not make things as easy for its owners as circus people have come to expect: it needs a substantial articulated lorry to transport it. Hence the size of the container-house is determined in the first place by the transporting capacity of the truck.

A House on Wheels. Johannes Kaufmann's Su-Si     Dimensions do not say anything about content. Su-Si is 12.5 metres long and 3.5 metres wide, but weighs 12 tons. You need an articulated lorry. After a delivery period of about four weeks the extravagant house from the Vorarlberg can be set up almost anywhere, either in an urban garden or on your lakeside plot. The slender living container fits everywhere, and does not insist on a particular use. Here a studio, there an office, exhibition gallery or second home. And if necessary, the designer house can move with you. Just heave it on to a truck and off you go. This ideal home for job-nomads shakes the very foundations of our little home-building culture. Not built solidly into the ground any longer, but almost something you can pick up off the shelf and put up in a trice. Attach power and water—and there you have it.

Su-Si, as in super-simple? That brings a grin to Johannes Kaufmann's face. He is the architect of the wooden container home, and he explains that his design is named after the first couple who owned it, Susanne and Siegfried. They wanted to live extravagantly, and to have

their own home, but they didn't even have a plot of land. Johannes Kaufmann got hold of that for them as well. He built the first Su-Si in autumn 1998, a highly polished break with convention. Coated timber panels on the outside, solid spruce inside. Su-Si consists of one room, with an area of 42 square metres. The bath is on one side, the kitchen counter on the other. Minimalism for real. Su-Si's advantages lie in the high quality of its finish. The timber structure with its large areas of insulated windows gives "super-good insulation values," says Kaufmann, and Su-Si would last for about 200 years, like "any good house," provided it is looked after properly.[5] The interior finish and fittings are chosen by the client, the lorry influences only the size. Because the whole thing comes from the factory in one piece but still has to be transportable, the construction had to respond to this, with additional reinforcement and material. Mobility comes at a price. And in this case it is at the expense of the lightness that this structure demonstrates so purely otherwise.

Johannes Kaufmann does not have to live by Su-Si alone. Fortunately, says the 35-year-old, who did his carpenter's apprenticeship in his parents' business, then trained as a structural draughtsman, took his master builder's examination in 1996 and his master carpenter's exam a year after that, before directing his practice in Dornheim with fellow architect Oskar Leo Kaufmann. Kaufmann now has his own architect's practice. The box has had a good dozen successors, mainly in the Vorarlberg. Only a few models went north over the Alps. Despite a positive critical response, Su-Si remains an exotic creature in the built landscape.

A wonderful sense of space: Su-Si has such a large area of glazing that it opens up to its surroundings, but it can also be closed off with curtains.

## Broom Dome, Lounge Tube or Bamboo Cube. Moritz Hauschild's Summerhouse Projects

Building is serious stuff. Producing something solid, durable, that you don't simply roll up or pack away. So what's all this: masses of bamboo, yellowish drainpipes and strips of corrugated polyester. And then there are some bricks and paddling pools. Props perfectly suited to a torture-chamber for architects. But there is a serious experiment behind all this: where does architecture begin? And what part can cheap, light mass-produced products play in this? "Open DIY hypermarket system" was the title of Moritz Hauschild's summer semester project for his students at the Technische Universität in Darmstadt in the year 2000.[6] There was method in the Munich architect's invitation to play with forbidden toys. The DIY store of all things, "a synonym for low-quality design and 'handicraft work' in detail,"[7] was to become a rich source for the architects of tomorrow. It was not really about the world of home improvers, it was about the treasures hidden there: materials, paints and surface textures that are largely unknown, that actually "should be in the care of an architect,"[8] as Hauschild puts it. As in his own projects, for which he uses unconventional materials, the Munich architect wants to impose limits—and then break the rules. The guidelines were demanding: every summerhouse had to be aesthetic, but it also had to be erectable within a week, with a minimum use of tools. It also had to stand up to wind and weather and offer rudimentary heat insulation. The little building had to be habitable for a year. Three completely different team designs crystallized out: Broom Dome, Lounge Tube and Bamboo Cube.

The Broom Dome project by Dirk Hennig, Julia Stefan and Silke Thron seems particularly mature. It is a dome construction à la Buckminster Fuller, except that the base lies flat. A load-bearing structure was assembled using a "broom handle-garden house combination" that ultimately exceeded all the expectations of stability. The construction and its envelope were built in only three days. The students pointed out self-critically that technically speaking working with foils made for untidy connections, despite rainwater- and UV-proof adhesive tape. They felt that an "off the peg envelope" would have "probably been worthwhile in terms of appearance and durability."[9] The Lounge Tube by Kai Merkert, Michaela Rothaug and Christoph Schuchardt was a striking, even spectacular manifestation: red, yellow and blue paddling pools are joined to make a horizontal cylinder, held together with heavy-duty sacks and pond liner, a colourful, mobile garden house for a season. In contrast with this, Martin Köhler's, Oliver Laumeyer's and Mira Sennrich's Bamboo Cube made of three metre poles fastened together with knotted rope seems almost conventional. The team hung a rope cube made up of a woven, translucent fabric tarpaulin in the framework. Hauschild calls the planned anarchy "breaking conventions open."[10] New approaches need stamina. But where do you begin, if not with the next generation of architects?

Buckminster Fuller would have been delighted. In the year 2000, students at the Technische Universität in Darmstadt developed a Broom Dome under the direction of Moritz Hauschild. It was built exclusively of materials that were available in the local do-it-yourself store.

For the Lounge Tube, tarpaulins and ropes were used to fit individual paddling pools together to form a pavilion 5.4 metres long. The paddling pools functioned simultaneously as a support structure, as foundations and as seating.

A house for Robinson Crusoe. The Bamboo Cube measured three by three by three metres. It was covered with tarpaulins and pond liner, and also builders' sheeting to make it rainproof. The bamboo structure was lashed together with ropes.

# Building a World of Bits and Bytes

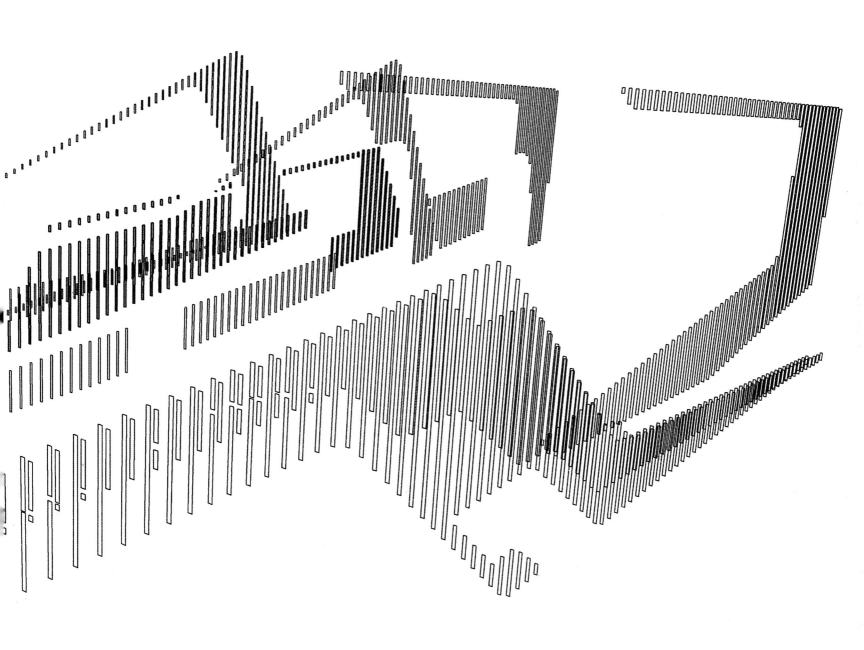

## Fluid Architecture from the Computer.
## Virtual Cities on the Net

In the last decade, software has changed the work of a profession concerned mainly with producing hardware more radically than most previous technical innovations. There has always been a field of creative tension between architectural vision and built reality, but the computer pushed the delicate balance towards improvisation and fantasy by opening up completely new design and presentation possibilities. Whole buildings are modelled on the screen today and designed down to the last detail, complex geometries are presented vividly and embedded in a photo-realistic illusory space that you can walk into and understand. Of course the cold light of current computer models is only the first step towards a second world that engages with the perception of so-called reality, and then outdoes it. Each new generation of computers blurs the boundaries between reality and fiction further: computers redefine materials. And not just as an aid and modern slide-rule, but as an "evolutionary accelerator and a generative force"[1] within the working process, even though in the new world of computers quality is not a question of RAM, hard disk size or processor speed, but remains linked to the creativity of individuals or teams.

Nought and one, the basis of our future information architecture,[2] become a digital admission ticket to the world of "Natural Born CADesigners," as Christian Pongratz and Maria Rita Perbellini called a group of young Americans, borrowing from Oliver Stone's film[3]: architects who consistently took advantage of the computer, using blobs and biomorphic shapes to break through the boundaries of the conventional world of right angles. At last, it seemed, architecture had also kept Heraclitus's promise and was flowing freely and effortlessly between the computers, without having to take on any final form.

◄ Flexibility thanks to the computer. State of the art machines made the system for Zaha Hadid's complex Mind Zone for Richard Rogers' Millennium Dome in London possible. An enormous range of design and realization phases were constantly checked over in this way.

A section through the Mind Zone shows the structure of the pavilion, which is reminiscent of the neuronal network of our cerebrum.

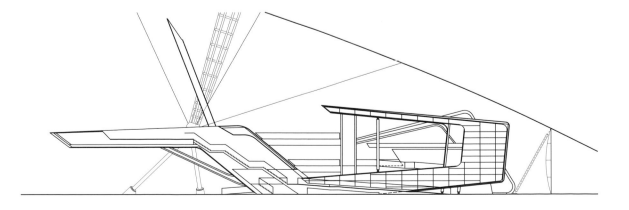

A highlight of Richard Rogers' Millennium Dome in London: Zaha Hadid's Mind Zone does not just play with unusual forms, but with unusual materials as well: aluminium honeycombs from the aviation industry and GRP (glass-reinforced plastic). This was backlit by fluorescent tubes.

## Place of Origin, the Computer. Zaha Hadid's Mind Zone in London

Zaha Hadid's Mind Zone in London is an excellent example of how the special features of a building commission can go hand in hand with the ephemeral aspects of its appearance. Just over a year after the exhibition pavilion in London's Millennium Dome opened, its last hour came as well. Hadid's impressive presentation of the human spirit was demolished in spring 2001, and all we have to remind us of this computer-generated structure are photographs, CAD drawings and project data. The project was as complex as it was fascinating. How, asked

Iranian-born Hadid, can you show something as abstract as thought without an open metaphor of this kind? The pavilion covered an area of 40 by 35 metres and had a support structure consisting of 360 tons of steel. It addresses the theme literally, and makes its extraordinary, abstract form into a container for artistic exhibits. To do this, Zaha Hadid created a three-dimensional continuum extending over several planes, linked by ramps and lifts. An envelope of transparent fibreglass panels gave the ribbon formed by the exhibition pavilion, which bent back into itself, both consistency and an almost magical presence. So despite its size the pavilion remained visually light, almost fleeting, as only thoughts can be. Even the support structure was rendered immaterial by the back-lit cladding.

Zaha Hadid used two approaches to perfect her Mind Zone, working with both models and computer animations that synthesized a number of design guidelines, for example the shape of the support structure and the material quality or appearance of its envelope. With her dramatic perspectives and powerful images in 3D Studio Max, Zaha Hadid held a trump card that she knew how to play when handing out commissions. The three-dimensional images formed a basis for the work of the structural engineers and Ove Arup and Partners.

In the course of time they had to introduce a number of changes for the objects inside, which kept the overall concept in flux for a long time and fitted in wonderfully well with the Mind Zone theme. We can only speculate about how this spatial experience that was designed so fascinatingly with the aid of computers would have turned out using conventional methods only. What is certain is that the computer was made an integral part in the design and working processes to a greater extent than ever before. After the built Mind Zone ceased to exist, the computer again became its location, as data files on a hard disk or in some other backup medium.

Sculpture in space or space in space? Zaha Hadid's dynamic Mind Zone faces the centre of the tent, but contrasts attractively with Richard Rogers' soaring roof.

Zaha Hadid answers the question about the optimum symbiosis of construction and form by making them both transparent.

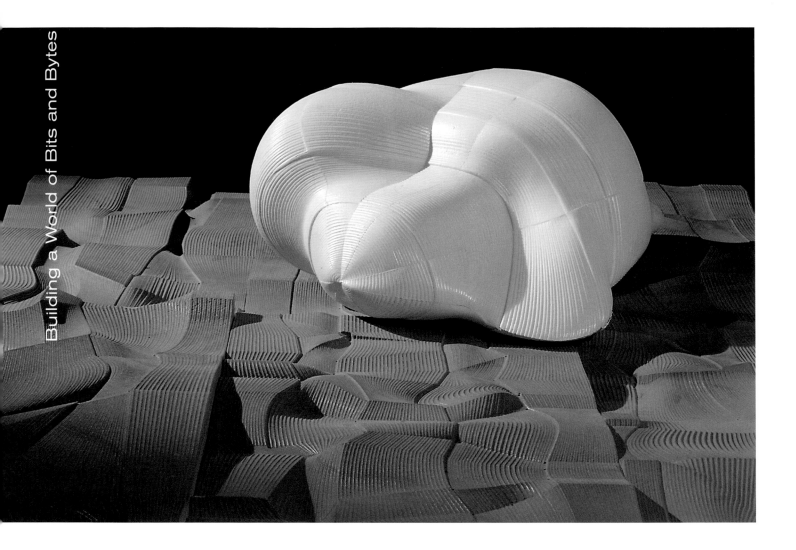

## Following Lined Paths. Greg Lynn's Architectural Animations

Where are the bounds of the brave new computer world, in which lightness seems to triumph over material, and ideas over execution? When space and time are only parameters within a computer model from Hollywood's special effects smithy, does it not seem a good idea to throw everything together for once to test out some new variants? In fact today's planners are able to follow a spontaneous suggestion and work it through realistically without moving a single stone. Linked computers enhance individual opportunities. CAD models, project data and images go off on their Internet travels—not the designers themselves. Small, decentralized teams work on large structures at the same time. Greg Lynn in Venice, California, Chicago's Garofalo Architects and Michael McInturf Architects from Cincinnati, Ohio showed how to do this with their Korean Presbyterian Church of New York in Sunnyside, Queens. Seven men in three different places designed a church for 2,500 believers. Thanks to linked telecommunications and animation programs from the American film industry, a former laundry of industrial proportions was successfully converted into a multifunctional culture centre with cafeteria,

The Korean Presbyterian Church in the New York district of Queens has been a new architectural highlight since 1999. It was developed by Greg Lynn with Garofalo Architects and Michael McInturf Architects.

Growing from the computer. Greg Lynn's Embryological House ©™ was created by high performance computers and film industry animation programs.

classrooms and meeting rooms. And just as the torpedo-shaped volumes of the original simulation finally developed into a real interior, the new contents changed the shape of the former factory, creating a complex interplay of forms. Avant-garde architecture had arrived in the industrial area of Queens, that until then had only been able to dream of Manhattan as a faraway setting.

Away from the building kit and on to open systems that transcend or redefine architectural types. That is what Greg Lynn is asking for, as he feels that the "highly developed artistic media culture increasingly enriches"[4] our imaginations. This architect, who was born in North Olsted, Ohio in 1964, redefined building and media quality by using Hollywood morphing programs as a basis for his own designs. Successfully. His computer-based Embryological House ©™ is already one of today's most famous mind games. What if a house were to grow and develop in a direction of its own, while remaining similar in principle? Greg Lynn examined this by giving his model individuality as well as a flexible, curvo-linear surface. Producing the pieces generated by the computer directly on CNC milling machines would mean giving a whole new meaning to the theme of the prefab and producing individual rooms and shapes using a similar data-base. Only one thing seems certain: architecture can scarcely get any faster or any lighter.

Six variations on a theme: tiny deviations from the six prototypes produce new and complex forms of Greg Lynn's Embryological House ©™ with its sensual bulges and curves.

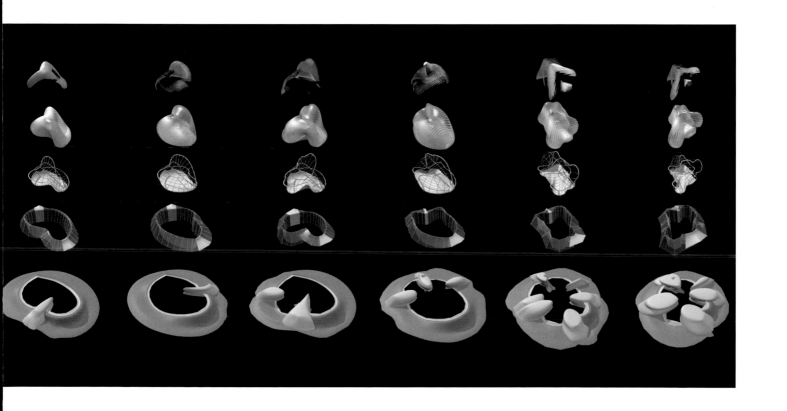

The Influence of the Exhibition. Bernhard Franken's BMW Pavilion in Frankfurt   "But the quintessence, the purest expression, the true reality of the design is its digital quality!"[5] says Bernhard Franken—and he seems to take a mischievous pleasure in his colleagues' astonished faces. His computer-calculated Clean Energy Pavilion BMW at the Frankfurt Car Show in 1999 enabled the architect, who was 34 years old at the time, to show want he wanted to derive from this for the built world: spectacular architecture. The model was the surface tension on two drops shortly before they fused together. Franken's pavilion was intended to be a sign of the car firm's new eco-consciousness and show the way to a new, powerful architectural language. Despite—or precisely because of—the fact that he uses high technology when seeking form, he is identifying a fundamental change: virtual architecture is trying to get close to nature. New—old—images are

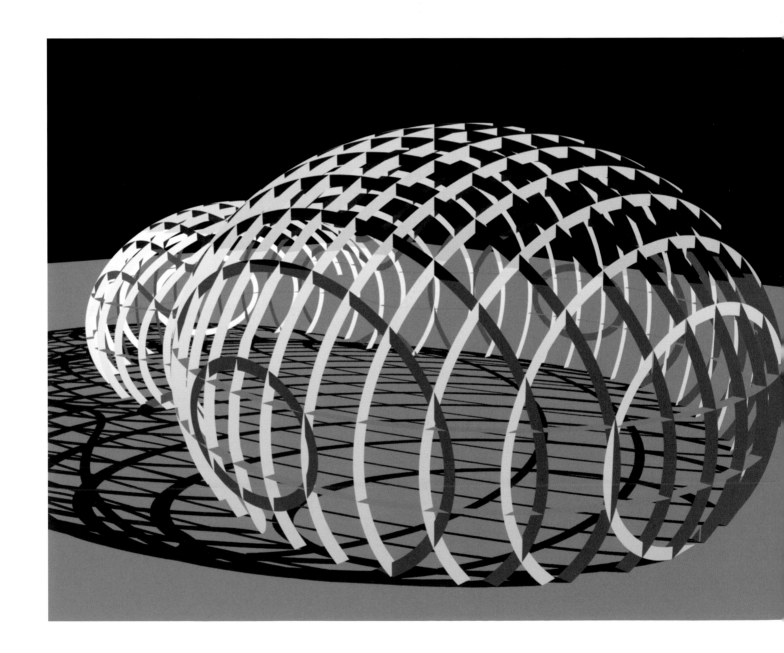

Bernhard Franken first prepared a computer simulation of the wire-mesh model of the BMW Pavilion for the 1999 Frankfurt Motor Show. He wanted to symbolize the moment at which two drops of water fuse together.

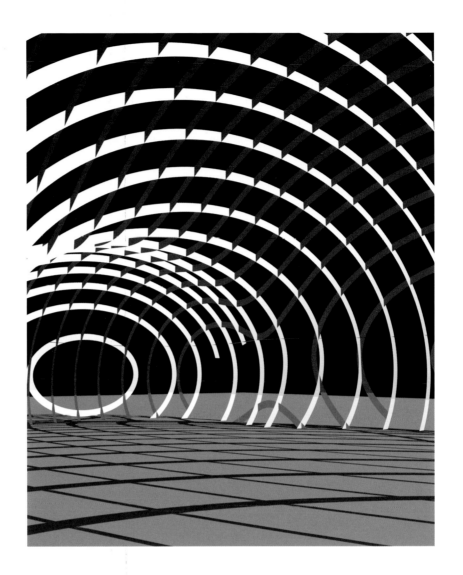

taking over the scene, unconventional ideas and forms that play with their constantly changeable form as though they were still animations, making the right angle seem like the gift of God to experienced critics. The arts pages have not yet decided whether the so-called Blobmasters, the choreographers of the new media aesthetic, are coming up with innovations that will last—or simply discomfort from the computer, as the horror film *The Blob* (from 1988) suggests.

Whichever way you look at it: the "liquid style" has conquered the architecture practices. The Blobmasters are increasingly coming up with substantial things from the realm of bits and bytes, powerful structures like Bernhard Franken's BMW Pavilion, which became the star of the 1999 Frankfurt Motor Show. An architecture of signs, representing lines of force symbolically and using them to instil form? Yes, of course! Data from the "wireframe models" we sent directly to the machine, and it turned them into tubes—support structures for the lightweight from the world of bits and bytes.

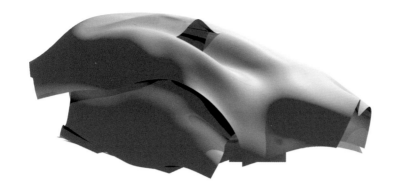

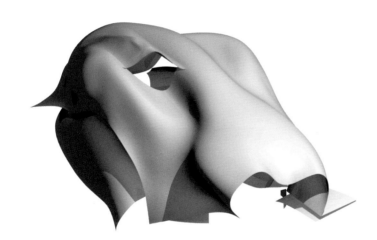

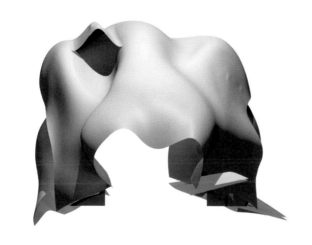

The old wizard Frank O. Gehry chose a different virtual development method for the conference room of the Deutsche Genossenschafts Bank in Berlin: first a little model was produced, called Horsehead; its data were fed into the computer, which then calculated the construction needed for the spatial sculpture.

## Fascinating Spatial Sculpture. Frank O. Gehry's Deutsche Genossenschafts Bank in Berlin

At first glance, the computer promises every possible freedom when designing. It is up to the architect to exploit this. Frank O. Gehry, the undisputed star of the sculptural architecture scene, squeezes the last quantum of performance out of his machine to create dynamic buildings. Their fascination does not lie in illustrating the best possible flow of forces or pure bodies, but a powerful, freely chosen form, without considering tradition or support structures. Artistic invention ultimately triumphs over material not least because engineers use their calculations to validate the formal tricks and bring them back into the realms of the feasible. The Guggenheim Museum in Bilbao proves how powerfully Gehry's spatial inventions can turn out. Its spectacular exterior transformed a whole city, making it into the Mecca of the architectural scene. In contrast, the Deutsche Genossenschafts Bank in Berlin shows that he can even do it without an undulating façade.

The Horsehead sculpture, now a reality in the atrium of the bank, looking like an outsize jewel in a showcase.

At first it is not possible to find any sign of Frank O. Gehry's characteristic undulating forms, no metal skin stretching and bending, no oblique angles in one of the most important—and historically significant—squares in Berlin, right in front of the Brandenburg Gate. An elegant façade stands on the site of 3 Pariser Platz, and behind it is hidden the façade of the bank. And yet: it is a genuine Gehry. Under the atrium, at the heart of the bank, things flash and shine: a freely formulated conference room under the great glass vault. The room itself takes the form of a dynamically winding spatial sculpture, and within it is an enormous sculpture rather like a silver-studded skull. The conference centre with its 100 seats is completely timber-clad inside—here too we have a valuable woodwork mosaic within the pattern of the city.

It first looks like an undulating metal landscape that can only have come from a computer in this form. Nothing could be more deceptive, as it is based on entirely conventional three-dimensional models made in the studio and only measured up and transformed into a lattice model in a second step. However incredible the spatial impression may be in the atrium and in the sheltering maw of the sculpture, nothing of this penetrates to the outside. The shock waves of the new shoot vertically up through the glass barrel, without being perceived by the city. A missed opportunity for Berlin?

Sharp edges, or are you a fluid person? Frank O. Gehry uses the roof of the Deutsche Genossenschafts Bank in Berlin to demonstrate how contrasts can be mutually enhancing, particularly when you remember the austerity of the façade.

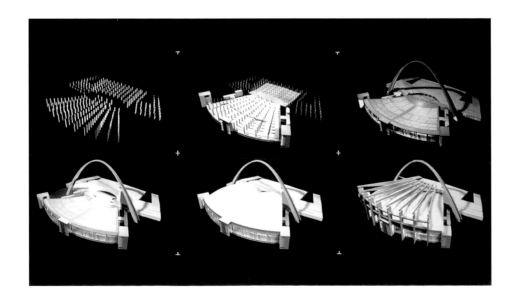

## The Art of Reconstruction. Johannes Herold's Archivision Project

The computer as a permanent research lab, with buildings and construction drawings for any particular moment—not entirely wrong as an idea. It is in fact all too easy for digital models to seem like construction matrices that have long abandoned any fixed condition, floating freely between the bits and bytes. And so it is only logical that the computer should help us to see the unrealized projects of the past. And that is precisely what Archivision is about.

Modernism has structural treasures under its surface that have yet to be excavated. The twentieth century's most famous designs are gradually reappearing, not tangibly, but as virtual structures or computer models. In the Archivision project, students from the Technische Universität in Munich are working on making it possible to see (and to teach) unrealized architectural visions. Johannes Herold's budding architects do not need any heavy equipment to do this. But they cannot manage without a sound working knowledge of CAD. Each project takes hundreds of man-hours. Mouse clicks and pull-down menus flood lattice models with artificial light. Bits and bytes represent concrete and steel, then glass and masonry. Textures stand in for tangible material. Finally it is possible to undertake a virtual guided tour, conveying a direct spatial impression. The animations do not create mere false façades, but meticulously researched models. How would Le Corbusier have constructed this detail? The architects constantly have to make decisions on the basis of known buildings. Reconstruction or productive copy? Sketches make interpretations possible. Ultimately the intention is that a few hints from the

Construction as a question of the right software: the students were able to reconstruct the building for the Palace of Soviet in several steps, build it up virtually and present in a realistic way.

The Archivision project
produced icons of architectural
history from the depths of the
computer: students at the
Technische Universität in
Munich associated with Frank
Herold and Marc Grellert
reconstructed Le Corbusier's
spectacular 1931 competition
entry for the Palace of Soviet
in Moscow.

architect—drawings, manuscripts and competition models—should produce
buildings that do not just exist on paper. Herold's list of projects starts with
Le Corbusier's competition entry for the 1931 Palace of Soviet, a spectacular design that was way ahead of its time. This is followed by Theo van
Doesburg's 1923 Maison Particulière and Walter Gropius's 1927 Total Theatre project. Giuseppe Terragni's 1938 Danteum is there, and so is Frank
Lloyd Wright's 1956 design for the futuristic Mile High Illinois skyscraper.
This reads like a Who's Who of Modern architecture, but it is based on very
precise selection criteria: the significance of the architect, the impact made
by his design and the uniqueness of his idea.[6]

Johannes Herold

## Looking for Lost Synagogues. Manfred Koob's and Marc Grellert's Virtual Reconstructions

Another higher education project linking contemporary history with architecture caused quite a stir as well: Manfred Koob's and Marc Grellert's exhibition *Synagogues in Germany. A virtual reconstruction*. Students from the Technische Universität in Darmstadt remembered the horrors of the Reich pogrom night of 9 to 10 November 1938, when over 1,600 synagogues were destroyed and 91 people murdered. The Nazis wanted to expunge from the collective memory something that had been expressed in architecture for a long time: the world of Judaism, with its places of worship and assembly. When another synagogue burned down in 1994, this time in Lübeck, it caused considerable alarm. Just under 50 students from the Technische Universität Darmstadt were not prepared to make do with expressions of dismay. They decided to rescue part of the past from being forgotten. Four Frankfurt synagogues were the first to be created on the screen. Ten more places of worship that had once been part of the townscape in Berlin, Cologne, Darmstadt, Dortmund, Dresden, Frankfurt, Hanover, Kaiserslautern, Leipzig, Munich, Nuremberg and Plauen were added in 2000. The students restored these synagogues that had been

Manfred Koob and Marc Grellert reconstructed several of the synagogues destroyed by the Nazis with their students at the Technische Universität in Darmstadt. The computer brought them back again, at least on a monitor: the towers of the Munich synagogue.

The interior of the Munich synagogue: a virtual tour of the computer models gives viewers a spatial impression that is very close to reality.

The impressive result of a detailed source study: here we have a view of the Cologne synagogue dome with its lavish ornamentation.

destroyed with the aid of computers. But even the most up-to-date CAD technology cannot replace historical documents. Where photographs and building plans had been deliberately destroyed or lost in the war, the source study moved into dozens of district surveyors' offices and municipal archives. However rigorously the students conducted their research and reconstructed lost material using typical construction elements and historical requirements, a great deal remained an approximation. "This can only convey an impression of how it was,"[7] said curator Agnieszka Lulinska of the Kunst- und Ausstellungshalle der Bundesrepublik in Bonn, where the results of the study were shown in the year 2000. A glimmer of hope remains: the project is continuing, and while old places of worship are at least being recreated virtually, real synagogues are being built again as well.[8]

## Virtual Spaces. Florian Raff's Exhibition Design

Nowhere, nowhere at all. Nothing but blackness. And in the middle of it all is the doorkeeper of the virtual exhibition world: a light grey monitor for you to click on. While a megabyte of data is being loaded the monitor remains dead. Then a corridor opens up, images flare up on the walls to the right and left, factory scenes and people in the street. The hand on the mouse feels its way further forward, the image zooms into a hall. Heads start to glow in the gigantic circle, as if on advertisement hoardings. The exhibition for the Internationaler Sozialistischer Kampfbund (International Socialist Alliance; ISK) takes us into virtual worlds.[9] The martial name hides an unjustly forgotten group that resisted the Nazis. The resistance workers used silver nitrate for their slogans, which burned them into walls and road surfaces. Its history has been accessible on the Internet since

Florian Raff's virtual exhibition world against forgetting the National Socialist past. The central rotunda contains linked portraits of resistance fighter from the Internationaler Sozialistischer Kampfbund (ISK).

In the digital gloom of the exhibition rooms only the programmers' spots illuminate the exhibits. The visitors click their way through various spatial sequences with their various textures and sizes.

18 December 2001, as a phantom made up of bits and bytes. Visitors move through this as if they are at a real exhibition. There is a front, a back, a right and a left. The difference is that the mouse determines the movements—not the head or the legs. This staging concept came from the exhibition maker Florian Raff, and it was implemented by Fa-Ro Marketing's web designers. Raff captured his ideal exhibition architecture in a sketch, free from the constraints of existing spaces. A nimble spatial sequence, quickly jotted down, that the web designers worked on for two months. Two months in which the concept was tested, questioned, and finally realized almost exactly as it had been. Although it is completely without substance, as bits indeed must be, the 3D world lost a considerable chunk of lightness. The rooms seem dark, inhospitable and claustrophobic, subterranean chambers that still have to prove their aesthetic quality.

## Views of the Future of the City 1. Bill Wright's SimCity—Town Planning for All

Landscapes at the touch of a button, cities from nowhere. And fluid architecture that is constantly changing, while seeming to shake off the bonds of time and material. And this is all thanks to the computer. It sets speed, chameleon-like changes and games against the world of gravity. SimCity, Bill Wright's game program for the home PC, removed even more boundaries and made ordinary citizens into town planners, creating big cities on the American pattern, with downtown, main roads and suburbs. The 1989 video game became a bestseller not because it presented us with a graphics revolution, but above all because it offered such polished games logic. A bird's-eye view of new worlds come into being, acceralerated. Single homes become blocks of flats and finally skyscrapers, provided the players ensure that their virtual citizens do not spend too long sitting in traffic jams and that the crime rate does not rise too rapidly. A complex situation made up of a few basic components—buildings and streets—rapidly emerges on a mapped landscape of your choice. It develops just like a real city, along with all the small everyday disasters like infernos and nuclear meltdowns, Godzillas and UFOs that reduce everything you have laboriously built up to rubble again. Professionals may smirk about playing around in this way, but even they could not manage without computers any more. CAD is the magic word, Computer Aided Design. The computer has caught up on designing with paper, pencil and drawing board, and already overtaken it in many places: from the tiniest detail to the complete whole, everything from the same hand.

Bill Wright's game program SimCity makes you both architect and mayor of a rapidly growing community—if you do everything right.

The typical American big-city grid, now on the computer screen as well—a new variation on the infinite planning world of computer games.

## Views of the Future of the City 2. Peter Haimerl's Zoomtown

Anyone going to the cinema and hoping to get an idea about the city of the future from science fiction films will be bitterly disappointed. There has never been a greater discrepancy between the hugely powerful simulation machines and the designers' feeble imaginations. Scenes from the *Thousand and One Nights* and sickly-sweet retro-kitsch flicker across the screen, regardless of whether the film is called *Episode 2* or *The Fifth Element*. Even in the world of Fritz Lang airships and double-deckers flit between the skyscrapers, which were linked together by walkways at a dizzy height. There is good reason for *Metropolis* being seen as the symbol of the ultimate city, even though critical voices were raised even at the première saying that the film was a cold, insensitive and shoddy effort made with exemplary technique, sentimental and undemanding. Visions age very rapidly. Very recently people accepted the idea of a virtual city in cyberspace that can be reached from anywhere via digital gloves and helmets. Today all that remains of these are ruined landscapes in video games, in which linked groups of players at LAN parties wage war, virtually but horrifyingly realistically.

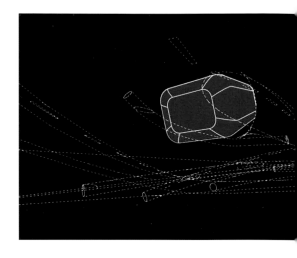

This "cargobyte" serves as an underground cargo-delivery in former subway tunnels.

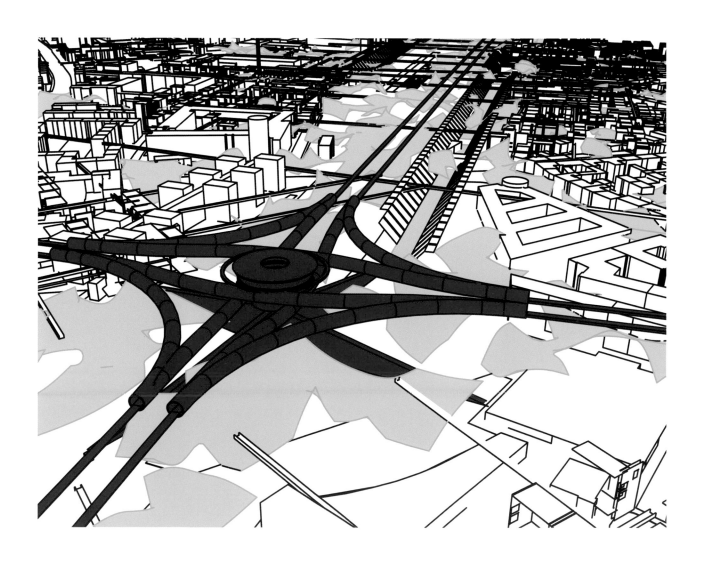

Environmentally friendly
vehicles like floaters and
electronic cars guarantee
mobility inside a district.

Virtual town planning used
professionally: Peter Haimerl's
Zoomtown links the cities of
Europe to make a single,
enormous meta-city. High-
speed trains link the individual
"districts" to London-
Barcelona-Berlin-Athens.

In contrast with this, the architect Peter Haimerl's vision of the
future is entirely pragmatic. His Zoomtown simulation shows how the most
important European cities could be combined to form a new meta-city
offering the best of all worlds. Haimerl conjures a "realistic" Utopia
out of the depths of his computer. This can be put into practice at any time
to stop "cities from expanding inordinately beyond their core."[10] The "Zoom-
liner" is waiting: it is a high speed transport system operating at up to
600 kph, linking cities like London and Barcelona, Berlin and Athens and
making them into parts of a single big city. City pilots surf around the
various sections of the city protecting resources with so-called floaters, in
which Haimerl includes conveyor belts as well as bicycles or electric cars.
Cars are scarcely needed any more, and citizens are winning the existing
inner-city road network back, building on it and planting greenery. The
usual antithetic structures like block peripheries and parcels or open and
green areas become less significant as the cities become denser and
greener at the same time. This is a necessary Utopia: 119 hectares of
nature are disappearing daily in Germany alone. Concreted over forever,
sealed and incorporated into the urban grid.[11] But while overdevelopment
is jogging cheerfully along in Central Europe, the cities of the Third and the
Fourth World are exploding. Of six billion people, half already live in cities.
There are 17 megacities with over 10 million inhabitants, and 13 of them
are in developing countries. There will be another nine by 2015. Conurba-
tions of this kind cannot offer a reasonable quality of life. Town planners
will not be able to do a great deal to prevent this growth. Can structures
of this size still be administered, planned and kept alive? If computers help
to keep the data together, offer simulations and thus make it easier to
arrive at decisions, then this hurtling growth process will have found a tool
to provide insights that works more rapidly than the process of change
itself. Simulation meets reality, at last.

143    Peter Haimerl

Architecture in Space

## Gracious Living in Space. Richard Horden's and Andreas Vogler's Space Design Project

An enormous doughnut spins majestically through space, a ring a mile in diameter. Ten thousand people live on the Stanford Torus space station.[1] We are in the near future, at least that is what NASA's plans said. They discussed the project with Stanford University in 1975. Even though there's no Blue Danube soundtrack, the influence of the science fiction film *2001: A Space Odyssey* can be felt down to the last detail in the orbital station. As in the film, the ring structure rotates around its axis, to simulate gravity in the interior. As in the film, Stanford Torus is still a building site: supply ships are buzzing around the outside skin, and astronauts are just fitting a new blind to the transparent tube. Around them there is nothing but the blackness of space, but a new world glows beneath them, a landscape rolled into place in zero gravity: rivers and woods, flowers and gardens, and in between you can make out real houses, bungalows exactly like the ones you might see on earth. An overwhelming panorama. "Still fantasy today, but it could become reality in the next century,"[2] a space travel expert was still joyfully proclaiming in 1979. A quarter of a century later, yesterday's dreams seem like leached-out transfers from an alien age, high-flown plans, becoming more colourful as the utter dreariness of space reality emerged. While the planners were waxing lyrical about small towns in orbit, the space travellers of those days were moving around in little tin cans, sucking their pre-prepared food from plastic bags and relieving themselves in their space suits. Not a hint of comfort, never mind design or architecture. Space was a world of bare survival, in which only technicians and doctors had a say.

"Houston, we've got a problem," said the Apollo 13 astronauts in April 1970: an explosion in the supply module threatened to abort their mission to the moon, and put the spacemen's lives at risk as well. Almost three decades later comes the almost equally laconic "Houston—we solve the problems." This time the slogan originated on earth, or more precisely, from a research project by the Technische Universität in Munich. Students from the building theory and product development department have been working on the interior design of future space stations like the International Space Station (ISS) since 1998. The problems are enormous; hitherto it has mainly been engineers who are responsible for space, rather than artists and designers. In space, in other words just a few hundred kilometres above the surface of the earth, 10,000 years of civilization seem to have been eradicated. Everything has to start from scratch. In contrast with the shiny science fiction images, ordinary things come first. No terrestrial chairs or tables function in space. Everything has to be tested and redeveloped to meet the dictates of zero gravity. This requires unconventional approaches and intelligent solutions, and the answer is often: form follows function. In the best cases, technology and design form a new alliance. Some of the problems seem almost trivial, as they are about basic needs

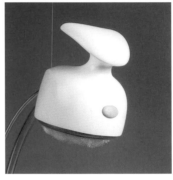

In space, even trivial everyday objects mutate into technological challenges: the PHA sponge that is being tested here was developed for the astronauts' daily hygiene.

The polyurethane sponge is supposed to be ergonomic and above all practical: the test model with in and out water supply tubes.

◄ A fascinating glimpse from outer space of the vast expanses of Greenland makes man's dream of another dimension all too understandable.

that we hardly think about on earth any more: how do you wash yourself when every drop of water goes into its own orbit? Can people sleep head downwards, or does it matter which way they face? When space missions lasted for only a few days it did not really seem necessary to design specially for zero gravity, or a mixture of brilliant improvisation and pragmatic restriction to what was absolutely necessary was applied, as on the Russian space station Mir. But this could become a problem if people spend long periods on the ISS. Everyday work will begin when the station is finally complete.

What is life like in zero gravity? And how are architects responding to the challenges posed by space even now? "From practice, for practice" is Andreas Vogler's motto. He works as an assistant in the British architect Richard Horden's academic department. Over two years, his students have become regular experts in space design, dealing with working and living conditions in space under zero gravity as though they had never done anything else. There were always improvements in detail to be made to the prototypes for the FLOW (Flexible Orbit Work Station) combined table and chair, the PHA (Personal Hygiene Assistant) sponge and the SpaceBed. This all started in 1998 as a two-terms design assignment on the subject of Space Hab (space station residential module), and it has now long gone beyond the bounds of a normal university project, both financially and logistically. Thousands of man-hours produced high tech solutions that surprised many space experts. When the students presented their project to NASA in March 1999 the personnel in the Johnson Space Center in Houston were impressed by the high design and technical quality of the work, Vogler explains.[3] They offered to test selected prototypes in parabolic flights, as close to reality as possible. Until then the students had had to make do with the Olympic swimming pool in Munich, using the buoyancy of divers under water to simulate weightlessness.

By the last week in October 1999 they had made it. Lecturer Andreas Vogler and seven of his students: Björn Bertheau, Claudia Hertrich and Arne Laub (FLOW); Bianca Artrope, Brigitte Borst (PHA); Thomas Dirlich (SpaceBed); Julia Habel (BOCS)—went on board the KC 135, Weightless Wonder V. They had a whole week of flying ahead of them, 160 parabolic flights in a specially equipped NASA jet. The four of them experienced something in their empty Boeing that is every normal passenger's worst nightmare: a nose-dive without power, creating artificial zero gravity for 25 seconds before the pilot takes control of the aircraft again and embarks on a new parabolic flight. Over and over again, 40 manoeuvres—and it went on for four days in succession. They were testing things like PHA, a polyurethane sponge intended to prevent water from flying freely around the space station as soon as someone starts washing, and the FLOW combined table and chair, intended to make everyday things like writing, reading and working at a computer easier. It is surprising at first glance. A pair of shovels unfold from the table-top on moving joints.

FLOW in use: the construction combines flexibility and stability in zero gravity, as confirmed by the first tested on ballistic flights.

The FLOW combination table and chair is an aluminium construction developed by students at the Technische Universität in Munich associated with Richard Horden and Andreas Vogler. It was intended to make it easier for astronauts to write, read and work at the computer.

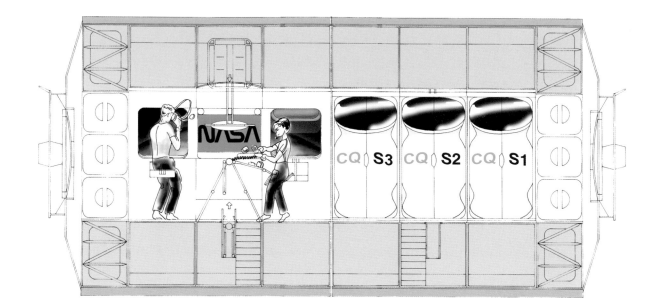

The testers fit their thighs and bottoms between these metal plates, so that they are sitting upright in zero gravity and can work on the table, which can also be moved. Why all this effort? Often a tiny movement is enough to set the astronauts floating through space. FLOW responds to the ergonomics of space and holds the astronauts in place, perfectly adapted to the so-called "neutral position" that the human body naturally adopts in space as a result of muscular tension: a foetal position, with the knees drawn up lightly towards the body and the arms floating freely at shoulder level.

FLOW, which in its—terrestrial—aluminium-rod version had looked more like a outsize children's toy than a precision apparatus, now had its baptism of fire behind it even before the flight. The correct seat, precision fitting and way the individual elements worked together had been tried out under water—in other words in conditions similar to space. This led to a flexible model in aviation aluminium, which could be adapted to a wide range of users with very few adjustments. A second version in solid steel had to be built for the flight itself, to meet NASA's safety requirements. Finally the model was equipped for maximum loads up to 2G (twice gravity acceleration!). While the plane was falling several hundred metres from a great height, NASA astronaut Mary Ellen Weber was trying out what it is like to sit down in zero gravity conditions, to fix yourself in position—and possibly to work as well. Her colleague Nigel Packham tested the PHA sponge that sucks up excess water and disposes of it via a tube. Astronauts regulate the quantity of water in almost the same way as in a terrestrial shower, by pressing a button on the end of the ergonomically shaped sponge. Both models worked successfully on the test flight.

Section through the spacelab in the belly of the space shuttle. The individual FLOW elements can be fastened together or used independently.

Gracious living in space—at the moment this is just a future dream for all the astronauts in the ISS, but perhaps it will soon be reality.

Designing for space means throwing any ideas relating to living on earth overboard. Weight and solidity have to be avoided at all costs, as every kilogram that has to be transported into space costs about 40,000 dollars. No wonder that even the NASA engineers thought of comfort last when designing the space shuttle. The design of the space station is intended to improve the astronauts living conditions considerably in all fields, from ergonomics to aesthetics. The fact is that architecture in space does not just mean working on details of how a shower or a desk might work. Architecture also means developing spaces for people to live in under zero gravity conditions. While the first space station modules were being shot into space and linked together in an ever-growing structure, the Munich department was working under pressure on what an ergonomic space habitat would look like: living, sleeping, eating, working, showering—everything is experimental and has to be reinvented or sensibly adapted to zero gravity conditions. Space travel technicians and architects are equally involved in a project of this kind for the first time.

The architecture studio on the first floor of the Technische Universität in Munich offers remarkable views of the cathedral and the Zugspitze, the highest mountain in Germany. And now eyes are turning upwards as well, towards the space station. "We are all learning what it means to build for space,"[4] Richard Horden explains. The Micro Architecture Unit Munich seems predestined for this work. Richard Horden's half poetic, half pragmatic motto "touch the earth lightly" is aimed at reducing building materials to a minimum and yet developing flexible, resilient architecture. The students have produced unconventional "micro" works like Silver Spider, a fragile metal framework using lightweight construction techniques for extreme Alpine sportsmen. It can claw itself fast between rock walls like a spider, and is then used as a base for climbs.

Micro-Gravity, building in zero gravity condition—takes up ideas from "Micro-Architecture" and develops them further, from lightweight construction to a complete understanding of how human beings respond in space. The planning is driven by holistic thinking, ecology in high-tech clothing. They suggest that this also explains the significance of space architecture for everyday life: "In future," says Richard Horden, "we have to learn to produce more with considerably less effort."[5] He adds that space simply acts as a catalyst. "A whole new aesthetic is emerging up there. Water glitters more delectably than any diamond."[6] And so it seemed a good idea not to hide the available stock of water away, but to keep it where the crew could see it—a glittering space showcase. The Munich leaflet about the ISS is intended to be inspiring as well. A white arrow is floating in space. "We are here," it says above it. And you can make out the earth as a gleaming blue sphere, accompanied by Venus and Mars, on their thin orbits around our central star. That's how simple it is, seen from space.

Tourists in space. A gigantic ring made up of empty external tanks from space shuttle missions forms the basis for a circular living complex planned by Howard Wolff; it will create gravity by revolving around its own axis.

## Room With a View. Howard Wolff's Plans for a Space Hotel

When Yuri Gagarin stepped into his Vostok 1 space capsule forty years ago, on 12 April 1961, he probably realized that this flight would give him a place in history. Gagarin's hop to a maximum of 327 metres above the blue planet lasted exactly one hour and 48 minutes. In subsequent years the Russians established one socialist endurance record after another with their space stations, but NASA had to fight rapidly increasing public apathy after its heroic moon programme. Obviously astronauts crammed into their tin cans were not the answer to the dream of infinite worlds. No wonder that constant cuts in NASA's budget are threatening to make the ISS into a "ruin in space,"[7] hurtling along at about 28,000 kilometres per hour. Given this, it is good that private individuals and companies are increasingly discovering space. The American architect Howard Wolff published plans for a commercial space hotel as early as 1999. His study suggested combining a dozen of the space shuttle's burned out fuel tanks to make a circular structure. Recycling in space. He intended to get a private orbital station up and running around 2017. Several billion euros for 100 paying guests experiencing a sunrise every one and a half hours about 300 kilometres above the earth—is this any more than a marketing gimmick? British journalists were among those the space hotel computer simulations reminded of Stanley Kubrick's film *2001: A Space Odyssey*. Wolff's plan suggests that the station should revolve once a minute, and even this would provide a quarter of a G (gravity), which would be fundamentally different from the zero gravity ISS. He does not anticipate that his only clients will be hard-boiled test pilots or scien-

There is zero gravity at the centre of the space hotel, and this is also the case in the two panoramic sections on both sides of the station. Anyone who has seen enough of the countless sunrises that occur daily can go off for a snooze in the ring's living accommodation.

tists, but normal tourists who don't get enough of a kick out of Caribbean cruises any more. Even if they expect a minimum of comfort and living conditions similar to those on earth they will look in vain for a room with a view. None of the twelve containers will have a window. There will be inflatable furniture inside, and the individual rooms in the tubes are not hard boxes, but will have soft walls. They are like parts of a gigantic orange segment in section. Though there is a minimum of gravity in the living containers, enough to sit down or take a shower, there is zero gravity at the centre of the wheel. There will be large viewing platforms at each end, spherical domes in specially hardened Plexiglas, intended to withstand even the impact of mini meteorites. Here the space tourists will probably all assemble and look down at the blue planet, half longingly and half in horror, perhaps thinking from time to time of the bungalow they have not paid off yet.

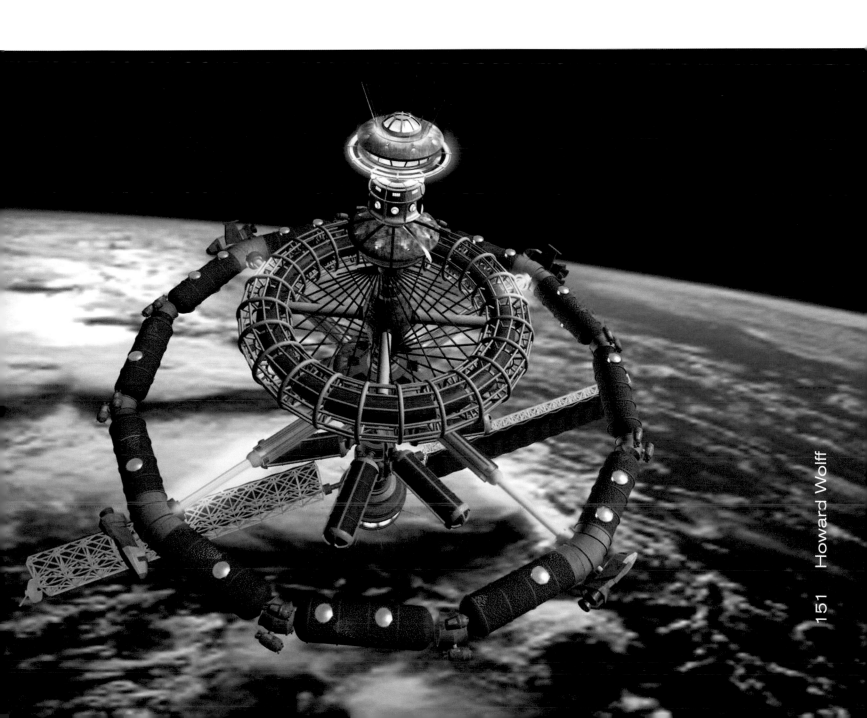

# A Little Featherweight Glossary

## Archi-neering

Neologism formed from "architecture" and "engineering," coined by the architect Helmut Jahn for his pioneering work with the engineer Werner Sobek. Anyone studying Modern architecture closely will come across a paradox: architects and engineers represent two disciplines that are mutually dependent but speak two different languages. Put plainly, the former concentrate on design, spatial sequences and questions of aesthetics and the others make sure that daring constructions stay up. Archi-neering shows that this division of labour, which suits both sides, can lead to mutual benefits.

## Bionic

Invented word combining "biology" and "technic(al)," introduced by J. E. Steele in 1958. It defines the interdisciplinary branch of science that examines natural structures technically, then uses the results to prefect artefacts that already exist or to create new technologies. Rudolf Bannasch defines bionics as a scientific discipline devoted to "decoding 'inventions by living nature' and using them innovatively for technical purposes."[1] For architecture this means finding the best possible evolved structures, forms and functions and translating them into improvements for support structures, envelopes and organization. Today scientists are working on decoding the adaptive growth of biological structures like bones and twigs, which will help to optimize the flow of forces and reduce the size of support structures in building. Engineers and bridge-builders have always proved that large spans require lightweight structures. Here the teacher is nature. It has been working on its concepts for adapting living things perfectly to the conditions on our home planet earth for millions of years. Its gigantic laboratory is open to anyone who is interested, indeed we are part (and the result) of these experiments ourselves. And so one strategy for lightweight architecture is "build on nature."

## Blob (Master)

Originally a derogatory name coined by Wes Jones for the generation of architects who made the computer into the key instrument in their design process. They used CAD techniques to develop free forms, partly using high-end software borrowed from Hollywood, that could not be produced, or could only be produced with difficulty, using conventional calculation methods. Virtual renderings and elaborate animations give a first insight into the possibilities of "fluid" architecture that can be parked on a local hard disk as a data-set or swapped, discussed and improved by e-mail on the Internet. Many computer-generated works break away from Modernism's right-angles and establish a natural, biomorphic formal repertoire based on expressive classics, called the "blob," with a hint of irony. Recently the works of the digital cyber-architects—the blobmasters—having become reality in a series of projects and thus have achieved a degree of conventionality. The Deutsche Architektur Museum in Frankfurt showed an extensive exhibition of their work in summer 2001.

## CAD

Abbreviation for Computer Aided Design, or more rarely Computer Aided Drafting. It is a construction and design method for industrial products, complete buildings or special applications using special computer programs, as a continuation and technical expansions of traditional architectural presentation using drawings or sketches. As well as Computer Aided Drafting, Computer Aided Design offers the possibility of working through the whole planning, design and construction process. Conversely, these procedures can be used to simulate buildings that were never built or reconstruct those that have been destroyed. And beyond these possibilities, the so-called blobmasters use computer architecture for new creative processes leading to lighter, more fluid architecture.

## Engineering

Engineers have always developed their structures from the necessities imposed by the material and the selected mode of construction. These objects are characterized by rational parameters rather than creative arbitrariness. As is shown by many bridges, the result often impresses with its extraordinary presence and high aesthetic quality. This does not so much apply to the Eiffel Tower, which simply took the vocabulary of the triumphal arch with an obelisk on top and magnified the dimensions enormously, as to Ferdinand Dutert and the engineer Contamin, who brought about an aesthetic revolution with their machine hall at the 1889 World Fair. The hinge-mounted support framework tapered towards the ground and reversed the ideas of load and load distribution. The hall had a span of 115 metres, and its bold forms and floating lightness made it the star of the show. Buildings like Renzo Piano's and Richard Rogers' Centre Pompidou in Paris, whose façade is derived directly from the visible structure and deliberately evokes echoes of lightweight industrial building, show how much the twentieth century engineering and machine aesthetic affected architecture.

## Exhibition Design/Set Design

No trade show can manage without it, no theatre and no rock concert. Nomadic and ephemeral structures and refined exhibition pavilions. Anything that needs to be mobile has to be able to be taken to pieces, and it must be easy to erect—anywhere. Or at least it has to look spectacular, like Bernhard Franken's Clean Energy Pavilion BMW for the 1999 Frankfurt Motor Show—blob architecture in its purest form: two drops fusing together. If this suggests reduction, the stage sets for modern rock shows are going in a completely different direction. Mark Fisher, who designed the massive sets for the Rolling Stones, U2 and Pink Floyd, knows all about this. Bigger, higher, more expensive. The set of Voodoo Lounge cost four million dollars, and it had to be built and struck again no fewer than 180 times in one year—an enormous logistic and structural achievement.

## Glass Architecture

Buildings consisting mainly of glass started to appear in the nineteenth century. These successors of the Gothic cathedrals, striving heavenwards with their high stained-glass windows, and of the eighteenth century orangeries were the outstanding monuments of the glass and iron industry. Cast iron and glass took over from solid masonry at the latest with Joseph Paxton's Crystal Palace in London (1851). Glass became the preferred material of Modernism. It was extraordinarily attractive, right down to the crystalline structures intended to blow the big cities open, as demonstrated by Mies van der Rohe's design for a glass skyscraper in Berlin's Friedrichstrasse in 1921. In Expressionism, coloured glass became a metaphor for the ethereal, transparency to higher levels of being—the "spiritual" element in architecture. Medieval mysticism and the twentieth century's dramatic sense of a fresh start came together in glass. Bruno Taut found an ideal and inspiration in Gothic cathedrals, the early Bauhaus revelled in analogies with a new tradition of masters and masons' guilds, and even sober engineers were intoxicated by so-called building with light. They wanted to create insubstantial space using immaterial resources, structures made up purely of colour, sound or light.

## Membrane

Thin, non-tear material that can be made of a textile of plastic foil, and that provides something that sounds impossible: large spans with a very low dead weight. It can be accommodated in minimal space and unfolded in the shortest time, it is translucent and has a number of qualities. Basic fabrics made of heavy-duty fibre (polyester or glass) are coated to make them UV-resistant or waterproof, breathable like Goretex or bulletproof like Kevlar. This built-in intelligence makes them ideal for use where flexible architecture is required or light envelopes for buildings that can wrap them up like a skin.

## Mobility

An important characteristic of portable, ephemeral architecture, like exhibition stands and tents. "Mobile homes" are a culture in their own right, particularly in the United States, from the VW Bully with its tent roof to the caravan that is chocked up on bricks when it is not going anywhere for a time. The idea of being here today and gone tomorrow is a continuation of nomadic culture, partly romantic, partly pragmatic, swapping the prescribed semi-detached idyll for a bit of freedom. Mobile accommodation also makes people prepared to have flexible ideas about where architecture begins. It is noticeable that there are a lot of pavilions around today, mobile structures that are built temporarily and soon disappear again, provisional facilities with a built-in sell-by date, conveying an illusion of a nomadic and easy life.

## Shell

Shell structures span large areas without intermediate supports. Shells disperse loads more effectively that traditional vaults because of their small volume, thus making it possible to construct extremely light, wide roofs with stable shapes. The preferred material is concrete. A distinction is made between single-curve shells like barrel and shed shells and double-curve shells like rotation, conoid, translation, paraboloid and hyperboloid shells. These "successors to traditional domes and vaults"[3] have extraordinary qualities. The membrane surface supports itself because of the double curve and can be made as an extremely thin shell. The master shell builders—Eduardo Torroja, Heinz Isler, Eladio Dieste, Félix Candela and Ulrich Müther—built on barrels, hyperbolic paraboloids and conical surfaces, thus creating extraordinary spatial innovations.

## Pneumatic

Inflatable structures with rounded organic forms, held up by their raised internal pressure and usually entered through an airlock. Alternatively, air cushions can provide a flexible outer skin for a fixed structure. The size of these extends from enormous exhibition halls as at Expo 1970 in Osaka to portable installations and furniture. Architects working around 1968 in particular used the revolutionary potential of this soft building method, which was so radically different from conventional approached. For example, Haus-Rucker-Co's performance apparatuses sounded challenging and ironic: their fragility was reminiscent of space suits and of the constant threat of love and togetherness in an age of commerce: Mind-Expander 1, a shell seat for two people with a PVC balloon that was supposed to open up a new view of the world by putting pink spots before your eyes, or a 1967 balloon for two that floated up high above Apollogasse in Vienna so that Maria Ebner and Stoff Superhuber could celebrate their symbolic engagement. The 1968 Yellow Heart was also supposed to beat rhythmically to the pulse of a new and better world. "Our balloons promote love," announced Haus-Rucker-Co, "we create apparatus that brings about and intensifies contact between two people."[2]

## Sketch

The first visual form taken by a creative idea. A symbol of lightness: floating, but not without substance, precise, but full of possibilities. It can be a drawing on a bistro serviette, a scribble in a notebook or a fluent CAD animation on a monitor. Things that are unbuilt and unbounded have always exerted an enormous fascination, particularly because they can be radical to the extent of breaking statical and constructional rules. Sketches open up architects' wishes like a fictional space, independent of concrete guidelines, clients or the limitations imposed by materials. Thus they can be the very opposite to a complete building—light and imaginative.

## Suspension Model

These made vault statics visible—and thus open to solution. A chain hangs down in the shape of a parabola, weighted at specific points to reflect the structure's thrust precisely. Thus the suspended chain corresponds to the ideal form of a vaulted arch in masonry—but standing on its head. A mirror above the model shows how the masonry for the arch actually has to be constructed. The catenary or tractrix was known even in the sixteenth century. The Dutch scientist Simon Stevin realized in 1585 that a weighted rope suspended at two points could provide information about the forces working on it. Master architects like Sir Christopher Wren, who built St Paul's Cathedral in London, right down to Antonio Gaudí (Sagrada Familia in Barcelona) refined this procedure for illustrating the interplay of forces.

## Tent

One of mankind's oldest and most universal dwellings. Portable structures consisting of a frame with an outer skin stretched over it. The skin can be made of leather, hide, woven mats, felt or woven fabric; modern tents use sailcloth or plastic sheeting, steel poles or plastics reinforced with fibre-glass; they are kept taut by guy-ropes pegged to the ground. There are various types: the ridge tent (North Africa to Tibet), conical tents (tepee; North America), house tent (yurts; Central Asia) and umbrella tents (toldos; Patagonia). This structure developed by nomadic cattle-breeders made a comeback in the nineteenth century—as a tent for circuses and celebrations. Frei Otto took up this great tradition in the twentieth century with his tent roofs, tent-like cable-net structures, in Montreal and Munich, though he used polyester and steel. Tents are now generally associated with living freely and close to nature in Western culture (camping), and they are also used as a practical solution when emergency accommodation is needed in disaster areas.

## Sustainability

This was originally a husbandry principle in forestry, laying down that no more timber should be cut than grows back on average. It is now used to describe environmentally-aware building with materials that conserve resources and use renewable energy when constructing and running a building. The demolition and disposal of the building are planned in. The principle applies to energy use and environmental factors in single buildings, and to the organization of districts and whole towns.

## Utopia

There were Utopian designs in architecture long before Thomas More's *De optime rei publicae statu deque nova insula Utopia*, published in 1516 and giving its name to the artistic genre. The idea extends from the Tower of Babel via Claude-Nicolas Ledoux's revolutionary architecture to Sant' Elia's drawings of the Città nuova and Buckminster Fuller's geodesic domes. A broad swathe of Utopian thinking runs through Modern architecture, from Giovanni Battista Piranesi's sequence of Carceri engravings via the fantasy architecture of Wassily Luckhardt (The Friends' Tower) to Bruno Taut, Frei Otto's town in the Arctic and the Archigram generation projects. They culminate in Bruno Taut's ideas of *Alpine Architecture* and futuristic machine cities that were never built, which makes them all the more effective in subsequent discussions. Finally, Utopian thinking is linked with the dramatic new initiatives taken in the 1960s, and the exponents of lightweight construction seeing the sky as the limit for their gigantic projects. Buckminster Fuller proposed an enormous geodesic dome over Midtown Manhattan to protect it from environmental pollution and nuclear threat, and in 1971 Frei Otto modelled a whole Antarctic city, covered with a translucent dome. Even Ron Herron's nimble Walking City of 1964 reaches dimensions far beyond technical feasibility.

## Endnotes

### The Weight of the World or: The Invention of Lightness in Architecture

1 Höller, Ralf: "Leichtigkeit als architektursprachliches Problem." In: *Prozess und Form 'Natürlicher Konstruktionen'. Der Sonderforschungsbereich 230*. Ed. by Klaus Teichmann and Joachim Wilke. Berlin, Ernst and Sohn, 1996, pp. 115–117, here p. 117.

2 The exhibiiton at the Vitra Design Museum was particularly highly thought of: *Living in Motion. Design und Architektur für flexibles Wohnen*. Ed. by Mathias Schwartz-Clauss and Alexander von Vegesack. Weil am Rhein, Vitra, 2002.
A number of technical journals devoted special issues to the subject, including "Der Architekt: Instant Architecture." *Der Architekt, Zeitschrift des Bundes Deutscher Architekten BDA*, 10 October 2000.

3 Kronenburg, Robert: *Portable Architecture*. Oxford, Architectural Press, 2000. (2nd Edition). And: Kronenburg, Robert: *Houses in Motion. The Genesis, History and Development of the Portable Building*. Chichester, Wiley-Academy, 2002. (2nd Edition).

4 Ludwig, Matthias: *Mobile Architektur. Geschichte und Entwicklung transportabler und modularer Bauten*. Stuttgart, Deutsche Verlags-Anstalt, 1998.

5 *Prozess und Form 'Natürlicher Konstruktionen'. Der Sonderforschungsbereich 230*. Ed. by Klaus Teichmann and Joachim Wilke. Berlin, Ernst and Sohn, 1996. See also a series of relevant titles like: "Ephemeral/Portable Architecture." *AD* Vol. 68, no. 9/10. September–October 1998.

6 Pawson, John: *Minimum*. London, Phaidon, 1996. For this see also another very readable book: Zabalbeascoa, Anatxu and Javier Rodríguez Marcos: *Minimalisms*. Barcelona, Editorial Gustavo Gili, 2000.

7 Zabalbeascoa, Anatxu and Javier Rodríguez Marcos: *Minimalisms*. Barcelona, Editorial Gustavo Gili, 2000, p. 90.

8 Joedicke, Jürgen: *Geschichte der modernen Architektur*. Stuttgart, Hatje, 1958, p. 153.

9 Conversation with Gernot Nalbach in September 2002.

10 Dessauce, Marc: "On Pneumatic Apparitions" in: *The inflatable Movement. Pneumatics and Protest in '68*. Edited by Marc Dessauce. New York, Princeton Architectural Press, 1999, pp. 13–26, here p. 13. Cf. also: Topham, Sean: *Blowup. Inflatable Art, Architecture and Design*. Munich, Prestel, 2002. And also: Bogner, Dieter: *Haus-Rucker-Co. Denkräume – Stadträume 1967–1992*. Klagenfurt, Ritter, 1992.

11 Conversation with Gernot Nalbach in September 2002.

12 Cf. Topham, Sean: op. cit., pp. 41 ff.

13 Conversation with Werner Sobek in September 2002.

14 Calvino, Italo: *Six Memos for the Next Millennium*. Cambridge, Harvard University Press, 1988.

15 Conversation with Frei Otto in September 1999.

### Building with Light. Bruno Taut's Glass Fantasies

1 Like the artistic avant-garde, Taut supported his work in the manifesto and enhanced its value. Bruno Taut wrote about 400 pieces, articles, manuscripts and "diary-like series of letters," cf.: Manfred Speidel: "Zu Bruno Tauts theoretischem Werk." In: *Bruno Taut. 1880–1938. Architekt zwischen Tradition und Avantgarde*. Ed. by Winfried Nerdinger and Kristiana Hartmann, Matthias Schirren, Manfred Speidel. Stuttgart, Deutsche Verlag Anstalt, 2001, pp. 396–403, here p. 396.

2 "Taut enriched twentieth century art literature with his published books, … but also with the magazine supplement 'Frühlicht, eine Folge für die Verwirklichung des Neuen Baugedankens', and with the form of the pictorial pamphlet. Thus he preceded Le Corbusier in exploding the forms of academic architectural theory …."
Schirren, Matthias: "Weltbild, Kosmos, Proportion. Der Theoretiker Bruno Taut." In: *Bruno Taut. 1880–1938. Architekt zwischen Tradition und Avantgarde*. Ed. by Winfried Nerdinger and Kristiana Hartmann, Matthias Schirren, Manfred Speidel. Stuttgart, Deutsche Verlags Anstalt, 2001, pp. 90–113, here p. 93.

3 "Taut, Bruno: Eine Notwendigkeit." In: *Der Sturm* 4, 196/197, February 1914, pp. 174–175.
"Faithful to the model provided by Nietzsche, Taut's temple was intened to represent his own expressive being, unhindered by descriptive or empirical reality." Whyte, Iain Boyd: "Der Visionär Bruno Taut." In: *Bruno Taut. 1880–1938. Architekt zwischen Tradition und Avantgarde*. Ed. by Winfried Nerdinger and Kristiana Hartmann, Matthias Schirren, Manfred Speidel. Stuttgart, Deutsche Verlags Anstalt, 2001, pp. 68–89, here p. 69.

4 Taut, Bruno: *Alpine Architektur*, sheet 10, Hagen i. W., 1919 (private print).

5 Scheerbart wrote a whole series of fantasy novels, for example *Liwûna und Kaidôh*, 1901, still conventionally called "a novel of the soul," whose leading character finally unites with a star, a piece of imaginary architecture. Finally, in the 1913 asteroid novel *Lesabéndio* the inhabitants of the asteroid Pallas, the Pallasians, try to unite themselves with a higher sphere by building a tower.

6 Thiekötter, Angelika, Matthias Schirn, Wolfgang Pehnt et al.: *Kristallisationen, Splitterungen. Bruno Tauts Glashaus*. Publ. by the Werkbund-Archiv Berlin, Basel, Birkhäuser, 1993, p. 46.

7 For this cf. remarks on the construction of Taut's "Fantasien": Krausse, Joachim: "Kosmisches Haus in Leichtbauweise. Bruno Tauts Glashauskuppel." In: Thiekötter, Angelika, Matthias Schirn, Wolfgang Pehnt et al.: op. cit., here p. 101.

8 Taut, Bruno: *Frühlicht. 1920–1922. Eine Folge für die Verwirklichung des neuen Baugedankens*. Ed. by Ulrich Conrads. Frankfurt, Ullstein, 1963, p. 19.

9 Taut, Bruno: *Glaserzeugung*, 1920, p. 10. Quoted from: Thiekötter, Angelika, Matthias Schirn, Wolfgang Pehnt et al.: op. cit., p. 25.

### Light and Heavy. Eero Saarinen's Trans World Airlines Terminal in New York

1 Eero Saarinen on his work. A selection of buildings dating from 1947 to 1964 with statements by the architect. Ed. by Aline B. Saarinen. New Haven, Yale University Press, 1962, p. 5.

2 Stoller, Ezra: *The TWA Terminal*. Introduction by Mark Lamster. New York, Princeton Architectural Press, 2002, p. VII

3 *Eero Saarinen on his work. A selection of buildings dating from 1947 to 1964 with statements by the architect*, edited by Aline B. Saarinen. New Haven, Yale University Press, 1962, p. 60.

4 Ibid.

5 Ibid.

6 Ibid.

7 Ibid.

8 Ibid.

9 Ibid.

10 Ibid.

11 Ibid.

### Geometry: Go and No-Go. Richard Buckminster Fuller's Visions

1 Fuller, Buckminster R.: "Einflüsse auf meine Arbeit." In: Fuller, Buckminster R.: *Bedienungsanleitung für das Raumschiff Erde und andere Schriften*. Ed. by Joachim Krausse. Dresden, Verlag der Kunst, 1998, pp. 168–211, here p. 194.

2 Ibid.

3 Kronenberg, Robert: "Moderne Architektur für variables Wohnen." In: *Living in Motion. Design und Architektur für flexibles Wohnen*. Ed, by Mathias Schwartz-Clauss and Alexander von Vegesack. Weil am Rhein, Vitra Design Museum, 2002, pp. 19–78, here p. 35.

4 Fuller, Buckminster R.: *Your Private Sky: Diskurs*. Ed. by Joachim Krausse and Claude Lichtenstein. Baden, Lars Müller, 2001, p. 90.

5 Ibid., p. 94.

6 Ibid., p. 93 and p.94.

7 Kronenberg, Robert, ibid., pp. 19–78, here p. 39.

8 *Prozess und Form "Natürlicher Konstruktionen."* Ed. by Klaus Teichmann and Joachim Wilke. Berlin, Ernst und Sohn, 1996, p. 105.

9 Krausse, Joachim: "Buckminster Fullers Vorschule der Synergetik." In: Fuller, Buckminster R.: *Bedienungsanleitung für das Raumschiff Erde und andere Schriften*. Ed. by Joachim Krausse. Dresden, Verlag der Kunst, 1998, pp. 213–306.

### Master of the Universe. Archigram's Pencil Revolution

1 Cf. the new edition in 1999: *Archigram*. Ed. by Peter Cook. New York, Princeton Architectural Press, 1999, p. 25.

2 Ibid.

3 Ibid., p. 61.

4 He was moulded by Robert Venturi's, Denise Scott Brown's and Steven Izenour's book: *Learning from Las Vegas*. Boston, MIT Press, 1978

### Escaping from Slab Construction. Ulrich Müther's Shell Artworks

1 All the following quotations are from personal conversations by the author with Ulrich Müther on 3 and 4 September 2002 in Binz, Rügen. Cf. also: Ed. by Winfried Dechau: *Kühne Solitäre. Ulrich Müther–Schalenbaumeister der DDR*. Deutsche Verlags Anstalt, Stuttgart, 2000, here particularly Weinstock, Kerstin: "Ulrich Müther. Vom 'Land-Baumeister' zum Schalenbauer. Bauingenieur-Porträt." In: *db* 10/99, pp. 152–160. And the article by Anne Urbauer: Urbauer, Anne: "Müther Superior." In: *wallpaper* 12/1999, pp. 73–78.

## Lightweight Construction

1 *Seifenblasen. Forming Bubbles.* Klaus Bach, Berthold Burkhardt, Frei Otto. Stuttgart, IL, 1987. (IL 18), p. 11.
2 Ibid., p. 6.
3 Ibid., p. 11.
4 Glaeser, Ludwig: *The Work of Frei Otto and his Teams 1955–1976.* Stuttgart, IL, 1978. (IL 17), p. 7.
5 Here two lightweight construction principles were juxtaposed: Otto's tent-like suspended roof structures with their long hawsers and Buckminster Fuller's massive domes, whose short, linked bars covered enormous spans. These structures have long been things of the past—only photographs remind us of these ephemeral giants—but one experimental structure with its characteristic eye-like opening to admit light has survived: Frei Otto's experimental structure, which later became the Institut für Leichte Flächentragwerke (IL), now 35 years old, and one of Baden-Württemberg's youngest listed buildings.
6 Nerdinger, Winfried: "*Kontinuität und Wandel der Architektur seit 1960.*" In: Pevsner, Nikolaus: *Europäische Architektur von den Anfängen bis zur Gegenwart.* Munich, Prestel, 1997, pp. 403–436, here p. 407.
7 Glaeser, Ludwig: *The Work of Frei Otto and his Teams 1955–1976.* Stuttgart, IL, 1978. (IL 17), p. 60.
8 Conversation with Werner Sobek in September 2002.
9 Ibid.
10 *Archi-Neering. Helmut Jahn, Werner Sobek.* Ed. by Susanne Anna. Hatje Cantz, Ostfildern, 1999, p. 46.
11 Ibid., p. 36.
12 Ibid., p. 39.
13 Ibid.
14 Conversation with Werner Sobek in September 2002.
15 Blaser, Werner: *Werner Sobek. Art of Engineering. Ingenieur-Kunst.* Basel, Birkhäuser, 1999, p. 7.
16 Explanatory text about R 129 on an in-house CD-ROM.
17 Sobeks search for the lightest possible load-bearing systems led to adaptive devices like the "Stuttgarter Träger," which accommodated actively to the current load, adapting through computer control. This made further quantum leaps possible, according to Sobek, between 50 and 100 per cent weight saving against traditional systems.

## Membranes and Light Materials

1 Conversation with Andreas Heller in October 1998.
2 Ibid.
3 Ibid.
4 Ibid.
5 Conversations with Benno Bauer in April 1999 and September 2002.
6 Ibid.

## Inflatable Architecture

1 Thallemer, Axel: "Luft verkaufen." In: *Gestaltung Macht Sinn, Macht Gestaltung Sinn. Internationales Forum für Gestaltung Ulm 2000.* Frankfurt/M., Anabas Verlag, 2001, pp.115–123, here p.119.
2 Glancey, Jonathan: *Nigel Coates. Body Buildings and City Scapes.* London, Thames and Hudson, 1999, p. 46.

## Modern Nomads

1 Luscombe, Belinda: He Builds With a Really Tough Material: Paper. http://www.time.com/time/innovators/design/profile_ban2.html
2 Conversation with Matthias Loebermann in October 2000.
3 Ibid.
4 Schnell, Angelika: *Junge deutsche Architekten/Young German Architects.* Basel, Birkhäuser, 2000, pp. 102–109.
5 Conversation with Johannes Kaufmann in December 2001.
6 Participating students: Nicole Bach, Peter Bäumel, Pia Breitwieser, Pamela Dirnhofer, Sebastian Grau, Dirk Henning, Anke Junker, Jean Kempf, Martin Köhler, Ruben Lang, Oliver Laumeyer, Tobias Mathijssen, Kai Merkert, Sven Pohl, Michaela Rothaug, Christoph Schuchardt, Christian Schwarz, Mira Sennrich, Julia Stefan and Silke Thron.
7 Conversation with Moritz Hauschild in December 2000.
8 Ibid.
9 Offenes System Baumarkt. Großer Entwurf Sommersemester 2000. Darmstadt, Technische Universität Darmstadt, Fachgebiet für Entwerfen und Hochbaukonstruktion II Prof. Moritz Hauschild, 2000, p. 118.
10 Conversation with Moritz Hauschild in December 2000.

## Building a World of Bits and Bytes

1 Pongratz, Christian, Maria Rita Perbellini: *Natural Born CAADesigners. Young American Architects.* Foreword by Antonio Saggio. Basel, Birkhäuser, 2000, p. 10.
2 Schmitt, Gerhard: *Information Architecture. Basis and Future of CAAD.* Basel, Birkhäuser, 1999.
3 Pongratz, Christian, Maria Rita Perbellini: *Natural Born CAADesigners. Young American Architects.* Foreword by Antonio Saggio. Basel, Birkhäuser, 2000.
4 Lynn, Greg: "Embryological House © ™." In: *Archithese* 2.02. March/April vol. 33, pp. 44–45, here p. 44.
5 Franken, Bernhard: "Aus Freude am Fahren. For the Joy of Driving." In: *Digital real: Blobmeister, erste gebaute Projekte.* Ed. by Peter Cachola Schmal. Basel, Birkhäuser, 2001, pp.184–189, here p. 184.
6 Conversation with Johannes Herold in June 2000.
7 Conversation with Agnieszka Lulinska in May 2000.
8 The department's work on the Internet can be seen on the site: www.cad.architektur.tu-darmstadt.de.
9 For history of the Internationaler Sozialistischer Kampfbund (ISK) see www.isk-muenchen.de
10 Conversation with Peter Haimerl in June 2000.
11 *Raumentwicklung und Raumordnung in Deutschland.* Ed. by the Bundesamt für Bauwesen und Raumplanung. Abbreviated version of the report. Bonn, 2001.

## Architecture in Space

1 Information on the Torus project under: http://www.l5news.org/stanfordtorus.htm and http://lifesci3.arc.nasa.gov/SpaceSettlement/75SummerStudy/Table_of_Contents1.html. Stanford Torus construction. Depicted are the final stages of installation of the radiation shielding. Painting by Don Davis courtesy of NASA.
2 Büdeler, Werner: *Geschichte der Raumfahrt.* Künzelsau, Sigloch Edition, 1979, p. 9.
3 All quotations from conversations in 2001/02.
4 Conversation with Richard Horden in April 1999.
5 Ibid.
6 Ibid.
7 *Der Spiegel* 46/2001.

## A Little Featherweight Glossary

1 Bannasch, Rudolf: "Forschen, analysieren, gestalten." In: *designreport* 9/02, pp. 20–25, here p. 20.
2 Bogner, Dieter: *Haus-Rucker-Co. Denkräume—Stadträume 1967–1992.* Klagenfurt, Ritter, 1992, p. 17.
3 Barthel, Rainer: "Form der Konstruktion—Konstruktion der Form." In: *Exemplarisch. Konstruktion und Raum in der Architektur des 20. Jahrhunderts. Beispiele aus der Sammlung des Architekturmuseums der Technischen Universität München.* Ed. by Winfried Nerdinger. Munich, Prestel, 2002, pp. 14–33, here p. 22.

## Selected Bibliography

*Archigram*. Ed. by Peter Cook. New York, Princeton Architectural Press, 1999.

*Archi-Neering. Helmut Jahn, Werner Sobek*. Ed. by Susanne Anna. Hatje Cantz, Ostfildern, 1999.

"Bannasch, Rudolf: Forschen, analysieren, gestalten." In: *designreport* 9/02, pp. 20-25.

Barthel, Rainer: "Form der Konstruktion—Konstruktion der Form." In: *Exemplarisch. Konstruktion und Raum in der Architektur des 20. Jahrhunderts. Beispiele aus der Sammlung des Architekturmuseums der Technischen Universität München*. Ed. by Winfried Nerdinger. Munich, Prestel, 2002, pp. 14–33.

Blaser, Werner: *Werner Sobek. Art of Engineering. Ingenieur-Kunst*. Basel, Birkhäuser, 1999.

Bogner, Dieter: *Haus-Rucker-Co. Denkräume—Stadträume 1967–1992*. Klagenfurt, Ritter, 1992.

*Bruno Taut. 1880–1938. Architekt zwischen Tradition und Avantgarde*. Ed. by Winfried Nerdinger and Kristiana Hartmann, Matthias Schirren, Manfred Speidel. Stuttgart, Deutsche Verlags Anstalt, 2001.

Dessauce, Marc: "On Pneumatic Apparitons." In: *The inflatable Movement. Pneumatics and Protest in '68*. Ed. by Marc Dessauce. New York, Princeton Architectural Press, 1999.

Digital real: Blobmeister, erste gebaute Projekte. Ed. by Peter Cachola Schmal. Basel, Boston, Berlin, Birkhäuser, 2001.

*Eero Saarinen on his work. A selection of buildings dating from 1947 to 1964 with statements by the architect, ed. by Aline B*. Saarinen. New Haven, Yale University Press, 1962.

"Ephemeral/Portable Architecture." *AD* Vol. 68, No 9/10. September–October 1998.

*Exemplarisch. Konstruktion und Raum in der Architektur des 20. Jahrhunderts. Beispiele aus der Sammlung des Architekturmuseums der Technischen Universität München*. Ed. by Winfried Nerdinger. Munich, Prestel, 2002.

Fuller, Buckminster Richard: *Bedienungsanleitung für das Raumschiff Erde und andere Schriften*. Ed. by Joachim Krausse. Dresden, Verlag der Kunst, 1998.

Fuller, Buckminster Richard: *Your Private Sky: Diskurs*. Ed. by Joachim Krausse and Claude Lichtenstein. Baden, Lars Müller, 2001.

Glaeser, Ludwig: *The Work of Frei Otto an his Teams 1955–1976*. Stuttgart, IL, 1978. (IL 17).

Glancey, Jonathan: *Nigel Coates. Body Buildings and City Scapes*. London, Thames and Hudson, 1999.

Höller, Ralf: "Leichtigkeit als architektursprachliches Problem." In: *Prozess und Form 'natürlicher Konstruktionen'. Der Sonderforschungsbereich 230*. Ed. by Klaus Teichmann and Joachim Wilke. Berlin, Ernst und Sohn, 1996, pp. 115–117.

Joedicke, Jürgen: *Geschichte der modernen Architektur*. Stuttgart, Hatje, 1958.

Krausse, Joachim: "Buckminster Fullers Vorschule der Synergetik." In: *Fuller, Buckminster Richard: Bedienungsanleitung für das Raumschiff Erde und andere Schriften*. Ed. by Joachim Krausse. Dresden, Verlag der Kunst, 1998.

Krausse, Joachim: "Kosmisches Haus in Leichtbauweise. Bruno Tauts Glashauskuppel." In: Angelika Thiekötter, Matthias Schirren, Wolfgag Pehnt u. a.: *Kristallisationen, Splitterungen. Bruno Tauts Glashaus*. Publ. by the Werkbund-Archiv Berlin, Basel, Birkhäuser, 1993, pp. 95–106.

Kronenburg, Robert: *Houses in Motion. The Genesis, History and Development of the Portable Building*. Chichester, Wiley-Academy, 2002. (2nd Edition).

Kronenburg, Robert: "Moderne Architektur für variables Wohnen." In: *Living in Motion. Design und Architektur für flexibles Wohnen*. Ed. by Mathias Schwartz-Clauss and Alexander von Vegesack. Weil am Rhein, Vitra Design Museum, 2002, pp. 19–78.

Kronenburg, Robert: *Portable Architecture*. Oxford, Architectural Press, 2000. (2nd Edition).

*Kühne Solitäre. Ulrich Müther—Schalenbaumeister der DDR*. Ed. by Winfried Dechau, Stuttgart, Deutsche Verlags Anstalt, 2000.

*Living in Motion. Design und Architektur für flexibles Wohnen*. Ed. by Mathias Schwartz-Clauss and Alexander von Vegesack. Weil am Rhein, Vitra Design Museum, 2002.

Ludwig, Matthias: *Mobile Architektur. Geschichte und Entwicklung transportabler und modularer Bauten*. Stuttgart, Deutsche Verlags Anstalt, 1998.

Nerdinger, Winfried: "Kontinuität und Wandel der Architektur seit 1960." In: Pevsner, Nikolaus: *Europäische Architektur von den Anfängen bis zur Gegenwart*. Munich, Prestel, 1997, pp. 403–436.

Pawson, John: *Minimum*. London, Phaidon, 1996.

Pevsner, Nikolaus: *Europäische Architektur von den Anfängen bis zur Gegenwart*. Munich, Prestel, 1997.

Prozess und Form "Natürlicher Konstruktionen." *Der Sonderforschungsbereich 230*. Ed. by Klaus Teichmann und Joachim Wilke. Berlin, Ernst and Sohn, 1996.

Schmitt, Gerhard: *Information Architecture. Basis and Future of CAAD*. Basel, Birkhäuser, 1999.

Schirren, Matthias: "Weltbild, Kosmos, Proportion. Der Theoretiker Bruno Taut." In: *Bruno Taut. 1880–1938. Architekt zwischen Tradition und Avantgarde*. Ed. by Winfried Nerdinger and Kristiana Hartmann, Matthias Schirren, Manfred Speidel. Stuttgart, Deutsche Verlags Anstalt, 2001, pp. 90–113.

Schnell, Angelika: *Junge deutsche Architekten/Young German Architects*. Basel, Birkhäuser, 2000.

Schock, Hans-Joachim: *Segel, Folien und Membranen. Innovative Konstruktionen in der textilen Architektur*. Basel, Birkhäuser, 1997.

*Seifenblasen. Forming Bubbles. Klaus Bach, Berthold Burkhardt, Frei Otto*. Stuttgart, IL, 1987. (IL 18).

*Shigeru Ban*. Ed. by Eugenia Bell. London, Laurence King Publishing, 2001.

Speidel, Manfred: "Zu Bruno Tauts theoretischem Werk." In: *Bruno Taut. 1880–1938. Architekt zwischen Tradition und Avantgarde*. Ed. by Winfried Nerdinger and Kristiana Hartmann, Matthias Schirren, Manfred Speidel. Stuttgart, Deutsche Verlags Anstalt, 2001, pp. 396–403.

Pongratz, Christian and Maria Rita Perbellini: *Natural Born CAADesigners. Young American Architects*. Foreword by Antonio Saggio. Basel, Birkhäuser, 2000.

Stoller, Ezra: *The TWA Terminal*. Introduction by Mark Lamster. New York, Princeton Architectural Press, 2002.

Taut, Bruno: *Frühlicht. 1920–1922. Eine Folge für die Verwirklichung des neuen Baugedankens*. Ed. by Ulrich Conrads. Frankfurt, Ullstein, 1963.

Taut, Bruno: "Eine Notwendigkeit." In: *Der Sturm* 4, 196/197, February 1914, pp. 174–175.

Thallemer, Axel: "Luft verkaufen." In: *Gestaltung Macht Sinn, Macht Gestaltung Sinn*. Internationales Forum für Gestaltung Ulm 2000. Frankfurt/M., Anabas Verlag, 2001, pp. 115–123, here p. 119.

Thiekötter, Angelika, Matthias Schirren, Wolfgag Pehnt et al.: *Kristallisationen, Splitterungen. Bruno Tauts Glashaus*. Publ. by the Werkbund-Archiv Berlin, Basel, Birkhäuser, 1993.

Topham, Sean: *Blowup. Inflatable Art, Architecture and Design*. Munich, Prestel, 2002.

Urbauer, Anne: "Müther Superior." In: *wallpaper* 24, 12/1999, pp. 73–78.

Weinstock, Kerstin: "Ulrich Müther. Vom 'Land-Baumeister' zum Schalenbauer. Bauingenieur-Porträt." In: *Deutsche Bauzeitung* 10/99, pp. 152-160.

Whyte, Iain Boyd: "Der Visionär Bruno Taut." In: *Bruno Taut. 1880–1938. Architekt zwischen Tradition und Avantgarde*. Ed. by Winfried Nerdinger and Kristiana Hartmann, Matthias Schirren, Manfred Speidel. Stuttgart, Deutsche Verlags Anstalt, 2001, pp. 68–89.

Zabalbeascoa, Anatxu and Javier Rodríguez Marcos: *Minimalisms*. Barcelona, Editorial Gustavo Gili, 2000.

## Illustration Credits

p. 16/17, 18, 19, 20   TU München, Munich
p. 22, 23, 24, 25   Bildarchiv Foto Marburg, Marburg
p. 26/27, 30   David F. Gallagher/lightningfield.com
p. 28   Institut für Leichtbau Entwerfen und Konstruieren (ILEK),
Universität Stuttgart, Stuttgart
p. 29, 32/33   Hubertus Adam, Zurich
p. 35   ILEK, Stuttgart
p. 36/37, 38, 39 (top and bottom), 40 (top and bottom), 42, 44/45
Courtesy, The Estate of R. Buckminster Fuller
p. 44   ILEK, Stuttgart
p. 46, 51 (top right and left), 50/51 (bottom), 52, 54/55
Archigram Archives, London
p. 48/49   Diana Jowsey/Archigram Archives, London
p. 56/57, 58, 63   Müther Archiv, Binz
p. 59   Klaus Ender, Bergen auf Rügen
p. 60/61   Kathrin Richter, Berlin
p. 62   Lutz Grünke, Binz
p. 64, 65   Bundermann, Berlin
p. 68/69, 70/71, 72 (top and bottom), 73 (top and bottom),
74 (top and bottom), 75 (top and bottom)   ILEK, Stuttgart
p. 76 (top and bottom), 77   Roland Halbe/artur, Cologne
p. 78/79 (bottom), 79 (top)   Werner Sobek Ingenieure, Stuttgart
p. 80/81   Florian Monheim/artur, Cologne
p. 82   Grant Smith, London
p. 83   detail from p. 80/81: Florian Monheim/artur, Cologne
p. 84/85, 86, 87   Klaus Frahm/artur, Cologne
p. 88, 89   Studio Andreas Heller GmbH, Hamburg
p. 90 (top)   Klaus Frahm/artur, Cologne
p. 90 (bottom)   Studio Andreas Heller GmbH, Hamburg
p. 91, 92/93, 93 (bottom)   Bernhard Friese, Pforzheim
p. 94/95, 96 (left), 96/97, 97 (right), 98/99 (top), 98 (bottom)
Festo Corporate Design, Esslingen
p. 100   Philip Vile
p. 101   Phil Sayer
p. 102/103, 104   Roland Halbe/artur, Cologne
p. 106 (top and bottom), 107   Hiroyuki Hirai
p. 108/109, 109 (bottom) right and left   Stefan Müller-Naumann, Munich
p. 110/111   Oliver Schuster, Stuttgart
p. 112, 113 (top and bottom)   Matthias Loebermann, Nuremberg
p. 114/115, 115 (right), 116   Ignacio Martínez, Lustenau
p. 119 (9 pictures)   Technische Universität Darmstadt, Darmstadt
p. 120/121, 122   Zaha Hadid Architects, London
p 123, 124, 125   Hélène Binet/Zaha Hadid Architects, London
p. 126 (top and bottom), 127   Greg Lynn FORM
p. 128, 129   Franken Architekten, Frankfurt/M.
p. 130 (top, centre, bottom)   Gehry Partners, LLP
p 131, 132/133   Roland Halbe/artur, Cologne
p. 134, 134/135   FLC/VG Bild-Kunst, Bonn
p. 136 (bottom right and left), 137   Technische Universität Darmstadt, FG
CAD in der Architektur, Prof. Manfred Koob, Darmstadt
p. 138, 139   Fa-Ro Marketing GmbH, Munich
p. 140/141, 141 (bottom)   Electronic Arts Inc. Electronic Arts, SimCity and
Maxis are registered trademarks of Electronic Arts Inc. in the United States
and other countries.
p. 142 (bottom), 142/143 (top), 143 (right)   Peter Haimerl, Munich
p. 144/145   Image courtesy of Earth Sciences and Image Analysis
Laboratory, NASA Johnson Space Center
p. 146 (3 pictures, top), 148, 148/149   Technische Universität München,
Munich
p. 146 (bottom)   Kayser-Threde GmbH, Munich
p. 150, 151   Wimberly Allison Tong & Goo (WATG) 2003

Every effort has been made to contact the copyright holders of photographs
and other illustrations. Any copyright holders we have been unable to reach
or to whom inaccurate acknowledgement has been made are invited to
contact the publisher.

The author would like to express his
utmost gratitude to the following individuals
and organisations:

Hubertus Adam
Benno Bauer
Allan Bell
Fa-Ro Marketing
Bernhard Franken
Dr. Inez Florschütz
David F. Gallagher
Marc Grellert
Peter Haimerl
Roland Halbe
Moritz Hauschild
Gabriela Heim
Frank Heinlein
Andreas Heller
Johannes Herold
Curt Holtz
Matthias Loebermann
Elena Manterolini
Graham Modlen
Ulrich Müther
Florian Nagler
Frei Otto
Kirsten Rachowiak
Fabio Ricci
Grant Smith
Lucien Smith
Werner Sobek
Maren Sostmann
Axel Thallemer
Andreas Vogler
Meike Weber
Iina Wilson
Howard Wolff

Oliver Herwig studied art history in Germany and in the United States. He works as a freelance journalist in Munich and was a visiting editor at *wallpaper** magazine.

*To Henriette*

© Prestel Verlag, Munich · Berlin · London · New York 2003
© for the text by Oliver Herwig
© for illustrations see Illustration Credits, page 159
© for illustrations on pp. 16/17, 18, 19, 20 (Bruno Taut, *Alpine Architektur*)
  Trustees of the estate of Bruno Taut

The title and concept of the "Architecture in Focus" series and
the titles and design of its individual volumes are protected by copyright
and may not be copied or imitated in any way.

Front and back cover: © artur / Roland Halbe, detail of Shigeru Ban's
Expo Pavilion in Hanover 2000, see pp. 104–107
Frontispiece: © Hélène Binet / Zaha Hadid Architects, London,
Mind Zone, see p. 125

Prestel Verlag
Königinstrasse 9, D-80539 Munich
Tel. +49 (89) 38 17 09-0
Fax +49 (89) 38 17 09-35

Prestel Publishing Ltd.
4 Bloomsbury Place, London WC1A 2QA
Tel. +44 (20) 7323-5004
Fax +44 (20) 7636-8004

Prestel Publishing
175 Fifth Avenue
New York, N.Y. 10010
Tel. +1 (212) 995-2720
Fax +1 (212) 995-2733

www.prestel.com

The Library of Congress Control Number: 2003102798

Die Deutsche Bibliothek holds a record of this publication in
Die Deutsche Nationalbibliografie; detailed bibliographical data
can be found under: http://dnb.dde.de

Prestel books are available worldwide. Please contact
your nearest bookseller or one of the above addresses
for information concerning your local distributor.

Translated from the German by Michael Robinson, London
Series concept: Angeli Sachs
Editorial direction: Kirsten Rachowiak
Copy-edited by: Curt Holtz
Design and layout: Meike Weber
Origination: ReproLine, Munich
Printing and Binding: EBS, Verona

Printed in Italy on acid-free paper.

ISBN 3-7913-2856-5